THE
SHAPE
OF
PREACHING

THEORY AND PRACTICE
IN SERMON DESIGN

DENNIS M. CAHILL

BakerBooks
Grand Rapids, Michigan

© 2007 by Dennis M. Cahill

Published by Baker Books
a division of Baker Publishing Group
P.O. Box 6287, Grand Rapids, MI 49516-6287
www.bakerbooks.com

Printed in the United States of America

Library of Congress Cataloging-in-Publication Data
Cahill, Dennis M., 1953–
    The shape of preaching : theory and practice in sermon design /
Dennis M. Cahill.
        p. cm.
    Includes bibliographical references.
    ISBN 10: 0-8010-6611-5 (pbk.)
    ISBN 978-0-8010-6611-5 (pbk.)
    1. Preaching. I. Title.
BV4211.3.C34 2007
251—dc22   2006030284

CONTENTS

FOREWORD

I have always wondered if I ever received a call to preach. When at sixteen I decided to be a preacher it was with motives both mixed and stained. I felt the tap of God on my shoulder, I guess. But looking back I wonder if my call was prompted by motives less noble. Good Christians attended church every Sunday, I knew, and perhaps I reasoned I would rather spend my Sundays up front speaking than sitting in a pew listening.

After I announced my "call," I was invited to speak to youth groups and preach in jails and rescue missions. It was all very simple. I prepared for those opportunities by grabbing a handful of tracts from the rack in the back of the church, then I memorized the stories and pieced them together into some kind of message, and finally I took the exhortation from a tract with its array of Bible verses to serve as the conclusion for my "message."

Adults in the church were impressed that a teenager could say something religious for twenty minutes and be somewhat interesting. I must have resembled a dog dancing on his hind feet. People are not impressed so much with the quality of the dog's performance as they are amazed that a dog could dance at all. At sixteen it all seemed easy. Preachers might not get paid as much as doctors or lawyers, I figured, but you certainly couldn't beat the hours, eleven to twelve on Sunday.

I did not realize then what I know now sixty years later. Preaching is hard work. It takes all of a person's heart and soul and mind to preach. No one spelled out the "mind" part to me. Had

I understood it, it might have derailed me. Hemmingway once commented that writing was easy. All you had to do was split open a vein, let the blood flow, dip your pen into it, and begin to write. I have felt that about preaching. Preaching can be a glorious experience. To stand before a congregation, believing that you have a word from God to tell them, ranks as one of life's glorious experiences. It's the "mind" part that can overwhelm you. The study, the thinking, and the preparation each week make preaching "a glorious burden."

It's hard to think. It's harder to think about thinking. It's hardest to write about thinking about thinking. Dennis Cahill has done just that. He has harvested insights about biblical preaching from many different people and from his own ministry, and put them together in this helpful book. In relatively few pages he walks us over the terrain we must travel as we think ourselves clear about the meaning and authority of the biblical text and how the passage affects different listeners' thinking and living. We owe him a debt of gratitude for what he has written!

But don't be deceived. While Pastor Cahill makes the process simple, he cannot make it easy. Thinking God's thoughts after him is demanding work. Communicating those thoughts to others is even harder. Yet certainly that work is part of what God calls us to as preachers. It takes all that we are and more than we have to carry it out successfully.

Haddon W. Robinson
Harold John Ockenga Distinguished Professor of Preaching
Gordon-Conwell Theological Seminary

PREFACE

I'm a pragmatist. I admit it. I want to know there is a payoff to what I read. I especially want that when it comes to preaching. I value books on preaching based on how much they help my preaching. How will some insight help me this week? "Don't just give me theory," I implore. "Don't you know I have to preach this week?" So my goal in this book is to give busy pastors something that will make a difference in this week's sermon. Or if not this week's sermon, I hope what I offer will at least be helpful with sermons in the near future. I want this book to be practical.

Questions of Theory

Sermon design is not just a matter of what works. Sermon design also relates to theology, literary form, and to the culture of the world in which we live. We cannot engage the discussion of sermon structure without entering into a conversation with issues of theory. The issues that relate to the form of the sermon are many and significant.

As I write this book, my oldest daughter, Megan, is in her first year of medical school, and my daughter-in-law, Katie, is in her third year of medical school. As best as I can understand it, medical school is a mix of practical training and theory. During the first two years much time is spent in the classroom and the laboratory. These two years provide a necessary foundation upon which the students' medical careers will be built. During the third and fourth years, most of their time is spent in hospitals. Students still attend occasional lectures, but most of the learning is hands-on. This book is divided up in much the same way. Part 1 is the theory and foundation upon which part 2 (the practical "how to") must be built.

So part 1 deals with issues of theory and theology and attempts to create a theological, literary, and cultural basis for making use of a variety of sermonic forms. This portion of the book attempts to create a foundation upon which creative approaches to sermon structure can be built. Throughout part 1 and especially its concluding chapter (chapter 6), I will argue that our sermon design must be evangelical (in accordance with the gospel).

Designing Sermons

We cannot ignore the practical issues of how sermons are formed, on which part 2 of the book focuses. In this second portion of the book, I try to deal with the all-important practical questions related to sermon design. This is the "how to" section. These chapters will help preachers to implement a discerning and varied approach to sermon form in their own preaching ministry. Perhaps more important than the actual forms we may choose to use is thinking through the process by which we arrive at form. Form is ultimately a product of how we *think* about text and audience. Learning to use new forms requires that we learn new ways of thinking about form and sermon. The goal of this book is ultimately practical—greater variety and ability in preaching the gospel to the world in which we live!

A Homiletic Journey

I invite you to join me on a homiletic journey. My own interest in sermon form grew out of my disillusionment with my own preaching ministry. My sermons seemed to be too much the same. "One size fits all" was my approach to every passage. But sometimes it seemed as if the text refused to be squeezed into my didactic mold. The literary form of the text cried "narrative," but its cry fell on deaf ears, for I knew only one approach to form. My journey began with lectures by Haddon Robinson at Gordon-Conwell Theological Seminary in the early 1990s. From him especially I learned a more flexible approach to the question of sermon structure. The journey has continued through my own reading, study, and faltering attempts at preaching. This journey to change has been difficult and slow, but I believe it has also been worthwhile.

Join me on a homiletic journey!

ACKNOWLEDGMENTS

I am deeply indebted to Haddon W. Robinson for the way he has shaped my understanding of homiletics. I was privileged to study preaching under Dr. Robinson at Gordon-Conwell Theological Seminary in the 1990s. It will not be difficult for the discerning reader to see Robinson's influence in the following pages. I have attempted to give him proper credit along the way.

I thank Timothy Slemmons, interim pastor at First Presbyterian Church in Titusville, New Jersey, and visiting lecturer at Princeton Theological Seminary; Kent Anderson, associate professor of applied theology at ACTS Seminaries of Trinity Western University; Randy Pelton, pastor at Calvary Bible Church in Mount Joy, Pennsylvania, and part-time faculty at the Haddon Robinson School of Preaching at Lancaster Bible College; Mark Baker, elder at Christ Community Church in Piscataway, New Jersey, and professor of linguistics at Rutgers University; and Mark Twombly, elder at Christ Community Church, for reading the manuscript of this book and making helpful comments. It was interesting to me that each brought a slightly different perspective to the task. I am also indebted to Rick Ravis, co-pastor with me at Christ Community Church, for the encouragement and advice about preaching that he has given me throughout our many years of working together.

I especially thank my wife, Patricia, who made numerous corrections as she read through the manuscript more times than anyone should have to. My thanks also to my son, Jonathan, my daughter-in-law, Katie, and my daughters, Megan and Sarah, for their encouragement in this project. Each of them found their way into the text by way of illustration.

And I thank my God who has granted me the wonderful privilege of preaching his Word to his people.

PART I

THE THEORY OF SERMON DESIGN

I read recently that the Leaning Tower of Pisa was closed for almost twelve years prior to 2001 to correct some of its lean. Officials feared that if the tower continued to lean farther each year, it would eventually collapse. The problem with the tower is not in its superstructure. The problem is with what is underneath. The soil on which it is built is not stable enough to support a structure of such magnitude. The problem is with the foundation.

The same can be true of sermon form. We cannot hope to wrestle well with the many questions related to sermon form (superstructure) unless we first attempt to deal with the foundational issues upon which various approaches to form rest. How can we hope to evaluate narrative approaches to form unless we understand the theological, literary, and cultural foundations upon which this approach to design is built?

This first part is devoted to just that: examining the underlying issues that relate to sermon form. In this portion of the book we will take a look at the ways sermons are formed; examine issues related to theology, literary form, and culture; and suggest an approach to form that is faithful to the gospel.

The impatient reader might want to skip ahead to part 2—and that is, of course, okay. (How could I stop you?) Yet I would encourage you to return to the first part before you are done, because part 1 is the necessary foundation for part 2.

1

Introduction to Sermon Form

Pastor Bill stares at the scribbling on a piece of paper. Finally, in frustration he crumples the paper into a ball and throws it at the trash can. It misses badly and lands among the other crumpled wads of sermonic effort scattered across the floor. It is a weekly struggle, this anguish of taking a passage of Scripture and turning it into a sermon. If only the Scripture came with a sermon outline attached! he laments. At times the structure of Sunday's sermon seems to just jump from the pages of the Bible, but at other times his attempts to find a series of preachable thoughts go nowhere. A sermon has three, perhaps four, parallel, distinct points—that is what he had been taught. And sometimes three or four points is just the thing—but at other times it seems . . . well, impossible.

His eyes drift to a journal on preaching that sits unopened upon his desk, a gift from a friend. "New Approaches to the Old Task," brags the headline. He should be working on Sunday's sermon, but instead he opens to the first page of the article. So begins his journey into the world of contemporary homiletic thought, a journey that will take him into contact with new approaches to homiletic design . . .

A new wind has blown across the homiletic landscape in recent decades, leaving behind new approaches to the old question of sermon form. Instead of the standard sermon structures of the past generations, preachers have begun to talk of fresh and innovative ways to communicate the old story. Sermon design has been the hot topic in homiletic literature for the last several decades. Terms such as *narrative preaching*, *inductive preaching*, *plot*, and *story* abound in the books and articles written on the sermonic craft. Eugene Lowry calls the new thinking on sermon structure a "paradigmatic shift."[1] Richard Eslinger has described the change in approach to form as "the Copernican Revolution in homiletics."[2]

It is, at first, almost surprising that the mundane issue of sermon form has so dominated homiletical discussion for the last three decades. For what could be less interesting than a sermon outline? What could seem less earthshaking than the order or arrangement of preaching ideas? Yet perhaps the new attention to form ought not to surprise us—for preaching is structural, and structure relates to every aspect of the preaching task. Sermon form relates to theology of preaching, sermon delivery, illustration and image, as well as biblical and theological content. "The power of a sermon," comments Halford E. Luccock, "lies in its structure, not in its decoration."[3] The thoughtful preacher who cares about communicating the Good News to today's generations can hardly avoid the issue of sermon form.

Sermon Form

Sermon form "has to do with the way in which the content of a sermon is proportioned and arranged."[4] The form is the skeleton that gives shape to the sermon. In my backyard is a swimming pool with a vinyl liner. Underneath the vinyl liner is a metal structure, which gives the pool its shape. That underlying structure is what makes the pool oval and not rectangular or kidney-shaped or L-shaped. Just as every pool has structure, so every sermon has form. Every preacher must make decisions about the kind of content to use as well as the order in which to deliver that content. The decisions we make in response to those kinds of choices are what constitute the form or design of the sermon.

Sermon form has to do with sequence: the order of ideas in the sermon. Which thought comes first? Which comes second? Which comes last? The order of preaching ideas is not a small matter in sermon design. A sermon is like a trip with one destination but with various stops along the way. Decisions must be made about the sequence of stops that will best enable the traveler to arrive at the final destination. Choices are unavoidable. If there are five main thoughts in a sermon, they must be spoken in a certain order—they cannot be spoken at once, at least not intelligibly. Thus every preacher orders thought. But, we wonder, why one order rather than another? That is the question of sequence.

Sermon form also deals with movement. Does the sermon move from the particular to the general or the reverse? Ralph Lewis tells us that there are only two basic thought patterns: inductive and deductive.[5] Some sermons reason inductively from the questions and struggles of life toward the biblical answers, while others begin with a biblical principle and move deductively toward specific life applications. The better preachers have always understood that a sermon needs to move. There must be progress in preaching. A sermon should never be static; it ought to go somewhere. A sermon is a journey toward a destination. Preachers must wrestle with questions of movement.

Sermon form relates to the content used in the sermon. Final decisions about the kind of content and the shaping of content cannot be made until the preacher knows where the sermon is going and how it will get there. The shape of the sermon affects the kind of material the preacher will use. A story sermon may be primarily made up of one or two stories. An inductive sermon may make great use of image. A deductive categorical sermon may deal mainly with argument. When preachers design a basic structure, a series of preachable ideas, they have the hooks upon which to hang the content of continued study.

The structure guides them as they search for sermon content and brainstorm for illustrations, images, and examples. Sermon form interacts with creativity. One of the great impediments to creativity in preaching is a prior commitment to one standard approach to structure. When a commitment to a particular form is made too early in the sermonic process, then creativity is limited. True creativity cannot be tethered to a single structure or approach to structure. It yearns to be free to associate, to relate, and to form in a variety of ways. The artist who believes there is only one way to paint will find little room for imagination and creativity. The preacher who knows only one way to form sermons will form sermons in just that way. The preacher's approach to structure will greatly influence the creative thinking-through process of sermon development.

Sermons have form. Preachers may find it difficult to give a name to the form of their sermon, yet their sermons do have form. Some sermons may use a deductive teaching pattern; others may be shaped with a narrative structure; some may be designed around a powerful image, but all sermons have form. The form of the sermon needs the same kind of intense and careful planning as the exegetical and theological aspects of the preaching task.

Traditional Approaches to Form

"Three points and a poem" is the not-so-kind caricature of the traditional sermon model. It is a model that has served well for many generations. The model can best be described as a thesis statement broken down into its relevant constituent parts. It is a structure that is remarkably suited to the communication of an idea or proposition. Indeed, the primary purpose of such a structure is to communicate a central thesis or idea.

The traditional sermon structure has its roots in Greek rhetoric and is the approach to form that was most often used in the pulpits of the first half of the twentieth century. The traditional approach is concerned with unity, parallel development, symmetry, distinction, and progression. Clarity and rationality are its preaching strengths. In a sense it is unfair to try to describe the traditional homiletical form as if it were a single structure. In reality, the traditional form allows for a rich variety of preaching. Thomas Long remarks, "Far from being predictable and uniform, the traditional approach to form in skillful hands produced a remarkable array of sermon structures."[6]

This is an approach to sermon form that worked well for many generations, and few questioned its homiletic wisdom. But with the coming of the final decades of the twentieth century, a rhetorical storm was brewing.

The Form Revolution

The attention of the homiletic world was captured by Fred Craddock's small book *As One without Authority*. Craddock, building on the work of David James Randolph who wrote *The Renewal of Preaching*, argued for a new approach to sermon form. With Craddock a major change occurred in the popular understanding of sermon structure. Craddock lamented the sameness of sermons in a rapidly changing world. With few exceptions sermons were rationalistic-deductive in form. In contrast, Craddock called for inductive movement.[7] While deductive movement goes from general truths toward the particular, inductive movement goes from the particulars of experience to the general truths of the gospel.

The inductive sermon does not announce its thesis at the beginning of the sermon. Rather the main thought is delayed as long as possible. In the inductive sermon, instead of the preacher telling the listener conclusions, the listener is invited along on the sermonic journey. The purpose of this sermon form is not so much the communication of information but the bringing about of an event. Something is to happen during the sermon time.

Craddock was soon to be followed by a host of homileticians writing on the issues of sermon form. Books and articles on narrative, story, and plot abounded. Many found in the new homiletics a new freedom. No longer bound by the restrictions of traditional form, preachers could soar wherever their creativity and imagination might take them.

Responses

The responses to the new approaches to form have been varied. Some have continued with business as usual—almost as if the revolution had never happened. Like flat-earthers on a round world, they continue with the status quo in a rapidly changing field. Week after week they ply their craft using a single approach to sermon design. The old tried-and-true structures learned in Bible college and seminary remain the staple in many if not most pulpits.

Others have quickly—sometimes too quickly—seen the light and adopted the newer sermon shapes as the "right" homiletical approach for newer times. Tired of the "same old thing," they have quickly taken hold of the newer approaches to the preaching task. These sermon forms have often seemed like a breath of fresh air, relieving the monotony of a pulpit that at times had become all too predictable. Unfortunately, those who make the jump to newer approaches to form often fail to realize the theological baggage that those forms of necessity bring with them (see chapter 3 for more on this).

Then there are those who don't know what to think (which may be most of us!). Uncertain which way to go, they go with what works. Their approach to form is essentially pragmatic. "This is what my congregation expects!" says one preacher. "But this is the method that works with today's generation," responds another. And there is a place for pragmatism. Yet our approach to sermon form needs a more sure foundation than just pragmatics. What is needed is serious consideration of the issues that relate to form.

As a young pastor, I recall talking with another pastor who had attended a seminary from a different theological tradition than my own. I recall hearing him tell me how he was taught to create story sermons. It all sounded rather strange. The preacher as storyteller was a new idea for me. Frankly, I didn't know what to think. I rather quickly dismissed it as a less-than-serious approach to preaching.

But new approaches to form are not so easy to dismiss. Homileticians from many different theological perspectives speak of story, narrative, and other creative approaches to the old task of structure. Haddon Robinson, Calvin Miller, Thomas Long,

William Willimon, and others have all weighed in on the debate over form. Preachers and homileticians of all sorts have looked anew at the shape of the sermon.

An Evangelical Approach

Thoughtful preachers concerned with effective communication cannot afford to ignore the newer homiletic developments. While we cannot simply adopt the latest homiletic forms without evaluating them and considering the sources from which they come, neither can these newer approaches be disregarded.

These new sermonic shapes cannot be captured under a single label. And they do not come from a single source. They are influenced by theology, theology of preaching, hermeneutics, rhetoric, culture, and literary criticism. The preacher concerned with being both biblical and relevant must enter into the dialogue about the newer forms, seeking always those that are faithful both to the gospel and to the listener. What is needed is an evangelical approach to form.

The question of sermon form cannot ultimately be a matter of either *status quo* or *going with the flow*. It is finally a question of communicating the gospel. That form which is evangelical (in accord with the gospel—the message of salvation through Jesus Christ) is a right form for any particular sermon.

All Christian preaching should be gospel preaching. Not that all sermons are evangelistic or that all sermons should be based on New Testament texts, but all sermons should find their focus in the gospel, the story of the life, death, and resurrection of Jesus Christ. The gospel is the theological center of Scripture. Sidney Greidanus states that to preach the gospel of Jesus Christ "is to proclaim some facet of the person, work, or teaching of Jesus of Nazareth so that people may believe him, trust him, love him, and obey him."[8] So all preaching should be gospel preaching. Whatever form we choose should be evangelical.

In 1 Corinthians 1:17 Paul states, "For Christ did not send me to baptize, but to preach the gospel—not with words of human wisdom, lest the cross of Christ be emptied of its power." Paul argues that the words and the form of preaching must serve to advance the cause of the gospel message. He is not contending against design or thoughtfulness in preaching but rather that the words and the design must not negate the message preached. No arbitrary standard, however notable and long its tradition, can be raised to determine the issue of form. The gospel itself must be our standard.

An evangelical approach to form will always ask first, Is this form faithful to the gospel? In answering that question, three issues must be considered: theology (our understanding of the gospel), literary form (the structure of the gospel in a particular text), and culture (those to whom the gospel must be communicated). These are the three winds—three forces of influence—that have shaped the discussion of form in our day, and they are the three issues that must be considered in developing an evangelical approach to sermon form.

2

THE SHAPES THAT
SERMONS TAKE

Pastor Bill stares at the yellow pad filled with scribbled notes, the result of a morning's hard study. Now he has to begin to design the sermon. This is the most frustrating part of sermon preparation—creating order out of chaos, giving shape to his thought. The journal article on preaching sits open on his desk as a reminder that there is more than one way to skin a sermon. From its pages he has heard rumors of inductive, deductive, narrative, and story. Fresh approaches to design fill his mind.

What would it look like, he wonders, if I tried a different approach this week? Maybe, he thinks, I can see this passage through new eyes . . .

P erhaps a journey into the world of homiletic design should begin with a description of the available options. The good news is that the number of approaches to sermon form is limited. These approaches, of course, are capable of almost unlimited variety and development. They are called by a variety of names. But there are only a few basic approaches. If nothing else, an awareness of the basic shapes that sermons take should make preachers more confident in the structure or structures they choose. And at best it may give them a greater variety and creativity in their preaching design. So we begin in this chapter with a discussion of the various shapes that sermons can take.

Classical Homiletical Form

In one sense the discussion of classical or traditional forms of preaching is almost unnecessary, since most of us have grown up listening to such preaching.[1] Many of us have heard countless sermons with three or four points, oftentimes alliterated, which might be labeled traditional.

The traditional form can be used with a fair amount of variety. Some preachers become predictable in their form, but the most skillful practitioners have used traditional forms with great diversity. Halford E. Luccock's textbook on preaching, *In the Minister's Workshop*, lists ten types of sermon structure, all of which could be described as variations on the traditional approach.[2]

There are several characteristics which unite these varied sermons under the single rubric "classical." So it is necessary to draw a few generalities, if only for the purposes of comparison with some of the newer forms. In doing so, we can make several broad statements of description.

Propositional in Its Purpose

Classical homiletics understands its purpose to be the presentation of a proposition. A main idea or theme is determined and the purpose of the sermon is to communicate that idea. Thomas Long explains that "in the traditional approach a sermon's form is crafted on the basis of the assumption that the task of a sermon is to present to the hearers a clear elaboration of some important idea or thesis."[3] There is no shortage of homiletical texts explaining the importance of finding the idea or theme of a text. The form of the sermon is then expected to explicate the proposition.

Deductive in Its Movement

Deductive movement (from the general to the particular) was not used exclusively in the traditional approach to homiletics. For instance, in *Design for Preaching* H. Grady Davis talks about inductive movement.[4] Yet deductive movement was the predominant plan for most sermon forms. This is because deduction is often the best way to clearly explain a proposition.

Rational in Its Feel

More distinctive than the movement of the form was its rational approach. Classical homiletics was predominantly rationalistic preaching. Argument and explanation were primary. The appeal was first to the intellect. Long describes Luccock's ten different sermon forms as all variations of traditional rational argument.[5]

Strengths and Weaknesses

The strength of the classical homiletical form was its clarity and its ability to communicate the doctrines of the church. Traditional sermon forms are especially useful for communicating information and ideas. That is why traditional structures are often used today in secular speeches that are designed to communicate information. Traditional forms continue to be used in many churches today with great effectiveness. The traditional form often fills a longing for biblical content.

For all its strengths, the traditional form has weaknesses. The traditional form often fails to connect with the form of the text itself. Often the literary form of the text is left behind in the process of sermon design. The genre of the text is engaged in the task of exegesis but discarded in the design phase. The form used for a sermon on the Letter to the Philippians might be the same basic form used for a sermon from the Gospel of Luke. The traditional form also often fails to connect with the listener. People live in a narrative world. That is especially true today. Inductive and narrative forms reign in modern communication. Television and film, two of the primary vehicles of modern communication, are essentially narrative mediums. Even the evening news attempts to tell stories. The attempt to reach the contemporary world using exclusively traditional forms may fail to engage the narrative character of our day (and perhaps of any day).

The approach to form that I took early in my ministry was fairly traditional. I would describe it as analytical. I would try to identify a main theme and then discover three or four thoughts about that theme. I would then put them in some kind of logical order for preaching. Sometimes it worked well and sometimes not so well. I noticed that some texts did not easily break down into three or four parallel preaching points.

For those reasons, and perhaps others, I and other preachers have moved toward less traditional forms of preaching in recent decades.

Inductive Sermon Form

A second form, which has gained in popularity in recent years, is the inductive sermon form. One basic distinction made by many (though not all) homileticians is the difference between inductive and deductive sermon structure. "Philosophers have found only two basic structures—inductive and deductive—for all human thought patterns."[6]

Fred Craddock's *As One without Authority* was a major catalyst in the move toward inductive preaching. In this slender volume Craddock espouses an inductive method of preaching. He was responding to a changing world in which the pulpit (in his view) had lost its power. He lists six reasons for the loss of pulpit effectiveness: (1) the minimization of the power of words to effect anything; (2) the mistrust of religious language; (3) the cultural changes due to television; (4) the loss of certainty and increased tentativeness of many preachers; (5) the new relationship between speaker and hearer; and lastly, (6) the difficulty of communicating in words.[7] All of this, according to Craddock, has led to a decline in the power and effectiveness of the sermon. The preacher can no longer carry an assumed authority into the pulpit. "No longer can the preacher presuppose the general recognition of his authority as a clergyman, or the authority of his institution, or the authority of Scripture."[8] Craddock's answer to the loss of pulpit effectiveness is the inductive method.

Inductive preaching, however, is not uniquely modern. It is not as though Craddock discovered something completely new. In the eighteenth century, François Fénelon proposed a homiletic method that was similar to the inductive method of today.[9] The problem/solution topical preaching of the 1920s was a form of inductive movement—moving inductively from problem toward solution. More recently, as mentioned earlier, Davis spoke of inductive movement in *Design for Preaching*.[10] But although inductive preaching has been used throughout the history of the church, the predominant form during most of the twentieth century was deductive preaching. Perhaps the best way to understand inductive preaching is to contrast it with the deductive method.

Deductive Preaching

In deductive preaching the sermon begins with propositions and attempts to prove, explain, or apply those propositions. Deductive thought begins with generalities and moves toward the particulars. In the deductive method the idea of the sermon (subject and complement) is stated in the introduction or the first point. The rest of the sermon is concerned with the explanation, demonstration, or application of that idea. Deductive preaching is rationalistic in its feel and linear in its logic. Deduction often features a categorical development, a development by analysis. The proposition, idea, or thesis is broken down into its component parts or categories. The strength of deduction is the authority of proclamation and the orderliness and logic of presentation. Deduction is a more direct form of communication than other forms and is generally more effective in conveying information and in teaching the doctrines of the church.

A typical deductive preaching outline might look like this:

Example of a Deductive Preaching Outline

Introduction
Body:
I.
   A.
      1.
      2.
   B.
II.
Conclusion

The deductive form has served the church well, and, when used properly, it has exhibited great variety and effectiveness.

Inductive Preaching

In inductive preaching the movement is reversed. Inductive thought begins with the particulars of life and experience and moves toward conclusions. Inductive preaching is concerned with the movement of the sermon. In an inductive sermon the subject is introduced in the introduction but the entire idea is not given. The sermon begins with the need of the listener and moves toward the answer of the gospel. Inductive preaching raises a question and then seeks to answer it. Whereas deduction tends to move in a straight line, induction is more likely to zig and zag. And although inductive preaching is logical, rather than the linear logic of deduction, it tends to make use of different forms of logic, such as contrast or cause-and-effect.

There are a number of distinct advantages to the inductive form. The inductive form creates interest. The inductive movement does this through creating a sense of anticipation or suspense, much as is done in a narration. Eugene Lowry says the most important element in a sermon is what he terms *ambiguity*.[11] Ambiguity is the uncertainty or unresolvedness of the sermon. There is a question that needs to be answered, a problem that needs a solution. Without ambiguity the sermon (whether inductive or deductive) will fail. Once ambiguity is introduced at the beginning of the sermon, the remainder of the sermon seeks to understand and resolve that ambiguity.

The inductive form elicits participation. The listener is no spectator; in the inductive process the listener is part of the sermon event. The inductive sermon is more of a dialogue than a monologue.

The inductive form respects the listener's ability to think and reason.[12] Inductive preaching expects the listener to follow the same thought processes that the preacher did in his study and invites the listener to come to the same surprising conclusion.

Craddock suggests that an inductive preaching outline might look something like this:[13]

Example of an Inductive Preaching Outline
        1.
        2.
    A.
        1.
        2.
    B.
    I.

Craddock is not seriously espousing such an outline, for it leans far too much toward the rational, logical movement that is characteristic of the deductive sermon. But it does help to show the difference in movement typical of the inductive method. The primary difference between deductive and inductive preaching is the kind of movement. Deduction is movement *from* while induction is movement *toward*. Characteristic of inductive preaching is that it is concerned with the descriptive more than the hortatory and with affirmation more than imperative.[14]

An important aspect of the inductive form is that in the inductive sermon the listener is expected to complete the sermon. The inductive process "calls for incompleteness."[15] The conclusion to the sermon is left open. This kind of sermon "respects the hearer as not only capable of but deserving the right to participate in that [inductive] movement and arrive at a conclusion that is his own, not just the speaker's."[16] Of course, the amount of incompleteness in an inductive sermon may vary widely. But the inductive process will allow the listener a greater part in the conclusion of the sermon.

This approach is seen in a sample sermon offered by Craddock titled "Doxology."[17] In the sermon, Craddock raises the question, "Is there ever a time or place when it is inappropriate to say, 'For from him and through him and to him are all things. To him be glory for ever. Amen'?" Craddock answers by telling of the death of his brother and the long ride to meet his now widowed sister-in-law. When he arrives he can think of nothing to say to her, but she breaks the silence with these words: "I hope you brought Doxology."

Craddock concludes the sermon like this: "The truth is now clear: if we ever lose our Doxology we might as well be dead. 'For from him and through him and to him are all things. To him be glory for ever. Amen.'" This sermon is instructive for it is a good example of what Craddock means by incompleteness. The listeners must complete the sermon by supplying those areas of life in which doxology must be included in their lives. But it is also important to note that this is not a completely open-ended sermon. For although Craddock leaves the listener some work to do, he does point them in a direction: doxology is essential in all areas and times of life. It is then left to the listeners to make application to various areas of their own lives.

Whereas the strength of deductive preaching is the ability to communicate information in a logical and rational manner, the strength of inductive preaching is its ability to involve the listener in the sermon event. Inductive preaching is especially helpful with hostile or indifferent audiences.[18] And inductive designs may be particularly appropriate for audiences who inhabit the inductive world of the twenty-first century.

Lowry warns that "the danger of deductive preaching lies at the end of the continuum where a sermon becomes mere report. The danger of inductive preaching at the other end of the continuum is where matters are so open-ended that people do not know what to do with the message."[19]

The Foundations of Inductive Preaching

Numerous issues relate specifically to the inductive form. The inductive method is first of all grounded in the shape of human experience. Induction is how people naturally live and listen. Much of life and learning is accomplished inductively. In general, we do not begin with conclusions and work toward particulars, we begin with the particulars and work toward conclusions. Learning is often a series of inductive discoveries. Modern homiletical development has shown a concern not just for the text but for the listener as well.

The inductive method is also based on the form of contemporary culture. We live in an inductive society. In particular this is true of American life. Americans have been raised on the inductive method. The inductiveness of life is especially evident in electronic media. Television is almost exclusively an inductive medium. Most television shows contain plots, not outlines. The change in contemporary oratory was seen in the 1996 Republican Convention, which instead of long speeches, made use of video, ten-minute messages, and narrative style to communicate its message. These changes in our culture demand a response from the homiletician. And the best response may often be using the inductive method.

The contemporary interest in inductive method also has its roots in the modern scientific method.[20] The scientific method is inductive in its approach: it begins with particulars and moves toward conclusions. This approach is reflected in the inductive sermon. The preacher engages in a scientific historical-critical study of the text in preparation for preaching. The inductive sermon then recreates the inductive exegetical process of the study. The listener is invited to participate in the journey. Craddock asks, "Why not re-create with the congregation [the] inductive experience of coming to an understanding of the text?"[21]

A further basis for the inductive method is the inductive shape of Scripture. For the evangelical this may be the most compelling reason to consider the inductive approach to preaching. The most common form of literature in the Bible is narrative, and narrative is inductive in its movement.[22] If the Scriptures themselves are largely inductive, it makes sense that the preacher would often employ the inductive method. The meaning of the text is intertwined with the form of the text. There is an indissoluble bond between meaning and form. Therefore faithfulness to the text requires that the form of the sermon should be suitable to the form of the text, and most often (or at least often) the sermon form will be inductive in nature. But all too frequently, Craddock notes, preaching "has its form defined not by the content of the Gospel nor the nature of Christian faith but by Greek rhetoric."[23]

Further, the inductive approach is grounded in the theological view that although humanity is apart from God, there is yet a point of contact between God and man. Here we enter into the well-known debate between Karl Barth and Emil Brunner over point of contact. Barth claimed that the Word of God was something wholly outside of human possibility. There is no point of contact. And if there is no point of contact, then concerns of rhetorical design are useless; there is nothing that either hearer or preacher can do to make the sermon more effective. The only course left is to preach the gospel and hope that God will break through to humanity.

Craddock sides with Brunner against Barth in finding a point of contact in the *imago Dei* (image of God), however tainted by sin. The image of God has been damaged in the fall, but not destroyed. Humanity is in conflict with God, says Craddock, but "a point of conflict is also a point of contact."[24]

Long makes perhaps the most compelling case for a point of contact by arguing from the existence of a God consciousness in humanity. That God consciousness is an evidence for a point of contact. Long asks, "Where did they get this God consciousness? Is it a remnant of the *imago Dei*—a memory of Eden built into the human frame, as Brunner suggests? Who knows? Preachers can remain conveniently agnostic about the origins of people's curiosity about God, but they cannot remain neutral about the fact that it is out there."[25] The reality of a point of contact is self-evident, even though the exact nature of that contact may be shrouded in mystery. Therefore, since there is a point of contact between God and man, it is often appropriate to begin a sermon with the needs of the hearers (an inductive approach).

The rise of the inductive form also reflects a shift in the understanding of the purpose of preaching. Many contemporary homileticians have questioned the traditional approach of communicating a proposition in favor of a more experiential and aesthetic view of sermon function. They have understood sermon purpose in terms of what a text is to do or, to borrow the terminology of David Buttrick, what a sermon "intends" to do.[26] This leads very naturally in the direction of inductive movement that is more geared toward creating a sermon event than toward communicating information.

Thus the inductive approach is grounded in Scripture, culture, and the listening event. The preacher, says Craddock, should choose a sermon form that is "congenial to the text, to the message of the sermon, and to the experience to be created."[27] That choice will often be inductive.

Inductive thought can be used in a number of different ways. The entire sermon can be structured inductively, as was Craddock's sermon "Doxology." The full idea of the sermon is not reached until the next to last line. It is also possible to incorporate inductive movement in individual steps of a sermon without making the entire sermon inductive, what Calvin Miller calls the "inductive lead."[28] Or a sermon might begin inductively, come to a conclusion, and then deductively explore the implications of that conclusion.

One need not look far to discover that inductive preaching is biblical. Much of the Old Testament is narrative and inductive in form. The parables of Jesus (a form of preaching) make use of inductive movement. And the New Testament epistles often employ an inductive approach.

It is equally clear that inductive preaching is culturally relevant. Inductive preaching is a particularly important mode of communication in the changing world in which we live.

But the inductive method should not be considered the exclusive form for preaching. In *As One without Authority*, Craddock is clear that he is not trying to make the inductive method the only method of preaching. Forms for preaching, he contends, should be as varied as the forms of Scripture.[29] The need of the congregation, the content of the text, and the purpose of the sermon may at times indicate that a more deductive form is to be preferred.

However, it is possible that for many contemporary preachers the inductive form will become the norm. The cultural changes in our society, along with the forms of the Scripture itself, will be a sufficient basis for many preachers to preach inductively much of the time.

Narrative Preaching

One form of preaching, which is primarily inductive, is termed *narrative preaching*. Narrative and inductive preaching are very similar, and at times identical. But the differences are significant enough to merit a separate discussion. John McClure notes that narrative and inductive preaching are sometimes confused since both are built around the delay of the preacher's meaning or idea.[30]

But narrative consists of more than delayed meaning. Lowry defines a narrative sermon as the arrangement of ideas in the form of a plot.[31] Narrative homileticians like to speak of sermonic plot. A plot is a series of events or movements presented in a particular sequence. The controlling metaphor for narrative homileticians is "creator of plots."[32]

Lowry sees a difference between narrative and inductive preaching when he notes that narrative may include both deductive and inductive thought.[33] Induction refers to the direction of the movement; narrative speaks of a sequence of events in the form of a plot. Narrative preaching does not simply mean that the preacher tells a story or many stories. The concern of narrative preaching is on the kind of movement in the sermon. "Typically, narrative preaching will embody a storylike process, moving from opening conflict, through complication, toward a peripeteia or reversal or decisive turn, resulting in a denouement or resolution of thought and experience."[34] A narrative sermon may or may not contain any particular story. And a sermon which contains many stories may not be a narrative sermon at all because of its nonnarrative structure.

Narrative preaching is an outgrowth of developments in biblical studies. In 1964 Amos Wilder published *The Language of the Gospel: Early Christian Rhetoric*,[35] in which he affirmed the unity of content and form in the biblical material. Wilder may overstate the case, because it is probably better to say that there is a relationship between content and form in the biblical material. Another influential work in narrative studies is Stephen Crites's essay "The Narrative Quality of Experience." Crites sees narrativity as the essential mode of human existence.[36]

These two works epitomize the twin foundations upon which narrative homiletics rest: (1) literary criticism with its emphasis upon the relationship between form and content, and (2) the narrative experience of life. Narrative structure is grounded in the shape of the text and the experience of the listener. These and other works were the soil out of which interest in narrative homiletics has grown.

The term *narrative* can be used in a variety of ways, which creates a certain amount of confusion. Lowry helps us to sort things out when he distinguishes narrative hermeneutics from narrative homiletics.[37] Narrative hermeneutics refers to a focus on the literary forms of the Bible and how those forms affect the sermon. Narrative in this case is a reference to the form of the text. Narrative homiletics refers to the use of the logic of narrative in preaching. Sermons in this sense are plotted.

Narrative is not just another sermon form among others but a different way of approaching the task of preaching. Lowry has described the paradigm shift from classical homiletics to narrative homiletics under three major headings. First is a shift in sermon shape. This shift is a move from deduction to induction, from an authoritarian relationship to a democratic relationship, from creed to hymn, from literality to orality, and from construction to development.[38]

The second major shift is the change in content. Lowry notes movement from discursive content toward aesthetic content. This is a shift in emphasis. Narrative preaching moves from discursive thought toward aesthetic content, but it will include both.[39] This is also a shift in content and includes a change from proposition to parable. Lowry explains what he means by parable: "Just as parable seeks not to make a point but to be one, so narrative preaching seeks not simply to report some extrinsic gospel truth, but to be the truth."[40] Just as a painting cannot be fully communicated through a propositional statement, neither can the gospel be fully communicated through propositions. Narrative communicates on a different and at times deeper level.

The third broad category of homiletical change has to do with the goal of the sermon. The sermon goal has shifted from theme toward event. "The goal of any sermon ought to be evocation of the experience of the Word."[41] In addition, there has been a shift from rhetoric to poetics. This is not an either/or kind of shift. Lowry asks us to imagine that instead of a rhetorically shaped envelope with poetics inside (illustrative and narrative material), that we now see a poetically shaped envelope with rhetorical ingredients inside.[42]

For Lowry the narrative sermon does not necessarily imply a narrative text. It turns out that the only texts on which Lowry does not use his standard narrative sermon plot are narrative texts since such texts have a plot of their own.

A narrative sermon, as Lowry defines it, does not mean the sermon consists of one story or a series of stories; rather the sermon should have narrative connectedness and movement. Sermons are to have plots—not outlines. In particular, the stages of a sermon should be (1) upsetting the equilibrium (oops); (2) analyzing the discrepancy (ugh); (3) disclosing the clue to resolution (aha); (4) experiencing the gospel (whee); and (5) anticipating the consequence (yeah).[43] In his newer work *The Sermon*, Lowry has streamlined his approach to four stages: conflict, complication, peripeteia (reversal or sudden shift), and denouement (resolution).[44] For Lowry, the primary goal in designing the sermon is to preserve ambiguity.

What is clear from all this is that classical homiletics and narrative homiletics are not mutually exclusive; there is a broad overlap. But it is equally clear that they constitute different ways of approaching the task of homiletics.

In defense of the narrative paradigm, narrative homileticians point first to the narrative character of Scripture itself. It is not that narrative is one form of Scripture out of many. Rather narrative is the normative form. All other forms, such as epistle, parable, or proverb, are meaningful only as they are related to the overarching narrative of the gospel.[45]

Secondly, they point to the narrative quality of life. We live in narrative. We all have stories. We all like to listen to stories. Preaching, then, is a matter of relating our stories to God's story. It makes sense that narrative would be the central paradigm for preaching.

The strength of narrative is the unity of sermon form with biblical form (when preaching a narrative text) and the appropriateness of this form for present-day culture. Its weaknesses can be a vagueness, an over-interest in aesthetics, and too much open-endedness. But I believe it is possible to utilize a narrative logic and still maintain the clarity which is essential for biblical preaching. Richard Lischer tells us that sermons operating from

a "rhetoric of promise" will operate "according to narrative logic
. . . [but] will never invest in the narrative form to the extent that
it is embarrassed by the language of direct address."[46]

I recently delivered a narrative sermon (a first person narrative in which the sermon is given from the perspective of one
of the story's characters). One of our church leaders, as he was
leaving, commented that the sermon caused him to think deeply
about himself. Such is the power of narrative.

Story Preaching

A particular variety of narrative preaching is called *story
preaching*. Lowry defines *story preaching* as a sermon consist-
ing entirely of a single story.[47] A number of authors espouse such
preaching, including Edmund A. Steimle, Morris J. Niedenthal,
and Charles Rice in *Preaching the Story*[48] and Richard Jensen in
both *Telling the Story* and, more recently, *Thinking in Story*.[49]

There has been a revival of interest in story in our day. Garrison
Keillor of *Prairie Home Companion* fame is popular because he is
a gifted storyteller. Practically no part of modern life is unaffected
by story. And story has deeply affected homiletics. The image we
should use for preaching, according to some homileticians, is that
of a storyteller.[50] It is not just that preachers should tell stories,
but that preachers are, in essence, storytellers. Story preaching
includes not only retelling the biblical story[51] but also the telling
of a secular story that parallels the biblical truth.[52]

And yet story preaching has its critics. Lischer has given a
sharp critique of story preaching in his article published in *Interpretation* entitled "The Limits of Story."[53] Stories, he reminds
us, are incomplete until interpreted.[54] Interpretation requires
discursive content. Further, stories unmediated by symbol and
principle do not effect transformation.[55] Lischer is not arguing
against story but rather against story in isolation from explanation and interpretation.

Long notes two weaknesses in the storytelling image for preaching. First, there is a tendency to underplay the nonnarrative aspects
of Scripture.[56] Significant portions of the Bible are nonnarrative.
The Bible does come to us with propositions and poems. The
storytelling image is not broad enough to capture the nonnarra-

tive character of Scripture. And then there is the danger that the preacher will simply become a creator of religious experiences.[57] Story preaching tends to move in two directions: toward the story of the text and toward our stories. There is the possibility that our stories will begin to overshadow *the story*.[58] William Willimon reminds us that the effort to tell our story can claim too much for our stories and too little for the biblical story.[59]

One often-ignored issue in the rush toward story is the continued success of more traditional modes of preaching. Regarding story preaching, Mark Ellingsen notes that "this sort of preaching . . . overlooks the success that fundamentalism and the evangelical movement have had even in our society of biblical illiterates. The emphasis on biblical basics seems to address a genuine need, rather than bypass a problem."[60]

There is still an important place at the preaching table for traditional approaches to sermon design. And yet there is also a place for story in our homiletics. But stories by themselves do not transform. Storytelling is insufficient as a controlling metaphor, and the sermon as story (a single story—either biblical or contemporary) is an insufficient vehicle to convey the full range of biblical truth.

Theological Approaches

We can address some of the drawbacks of story preaching if we remember that we can take a more theological approach to the question of form. A number of homileticians form their sermons using a theological template. Paul Scott Wilson uses an explicitly theological approach to the design of the sermon in *The Four Pages of the Sermon*. He rephrases the theological categories of law and gospel as trouble and grace. Every text should include a "theological movement from brokenness and trouble to restoration and grace."[61] His four pages of the sermon are a metaphor for four movements of the sermon. The first two have to do with "trouble"—trouble in the Bible and trouble in the world. The second two pages deal with grace in the Bible and grace in the world.[62] Although the order of the four pages may be shifted, every sermon should contain all four pages. This approach is captured in the words of Frederick Buechner: "The Gospel is bad news before it is good news."[63]

Bryan Chapell makes a strong case for taking a theological perspective to the development of sermons. His concept of the *Fallen Condition Focus* (FCF) along with the *redemptive approach* to preaching give guidance for the organization of the sermon. He tells us that the FCF is "the mutual human condition that contemporary believers share with those to or about whom the text was written that requires the grace of the passage for God's people to glorify and enjoy him."[64] The FCF gives us the "so what?" of the passage. That combined with what Chapell calls the "redemptive purpose" of the text will help the preacher design the sermon. The FCF is raised in the introduction of the sermon, and the body of the sermon responds to the FCF by giving the redemptive purpose.[65]

I used a theological structure in designing a sermon on Ephesians 5:1–2. In the first two points I introduced trouble: we are to live a life of love and a life of love is costly. It was trouble because in ourselves we are not able to live such a life. My next point introduced grace: we have been loved (v. 1b). Because we have been loved in Christ, we can now love. And then in my last two points I showed how we are to respond to grace by loving others and offering to God the sacrifice of a life lived in love. In terms of theological structure, it went from trouble, to grace, to the response of obedience.

A theological approach can be particularly helpful when we are trying to preach inductively. Begin with the trouble in the passage (the FCF), move toward its resolution in the gospel (the redemptive purpose), and conclude with our response to grace.

David Buttrick and Sermon Form

Perhaps the major contemporary text having to do with sermon form is David Buttrick's massive *Homiletic*. It is major not only in terms of its bulk (almost five hundred pages) but because of the significant new approach that Buttrick took to the task of homiletics. The book divides into two parts: the first section deals with *moves*, "a study of the components of sermons,"[66] and the second part explains *structure*, which has to do with the overall design of sermons.

Move is a Buttrick term for what normally has been called in classical homiletics a *point*. The term *move* is used to stress the movement of thought in the sermon. For, as Buttrick points out, sermons are a movement of language "from one idea to another."[67]

Buttrick attempts to understand the preaching event in terms of its effect upon human consciousness. The sermon consists of a series of concise, self-contained, yet connected moves, which together form an intentional whole in the consciousness of the listener. Much as a filmstrip consists of individual pictures, which viewed together form a single moving image in the consciousness of the viewer, so a series of moves forms a single whole in the mind of the listener.

The strength of Buttrick's work is his specificity. Buttrick is nothing if not definite. A move should last no longer than four minutes,[68] begin with an opening statement, which should consist of several sentences,[69] and should be closed with a restatement of the opening statement.[70] An opening statement should show *connective logic* and *point of view* (the relation of the hearer to the move) and must set the *mood* of the move.[71]

Buttrick is also very careful in his development of moves. Moves have three functions: they bring out theology, they associate, and they disassociate.[72] And a rightly designed move will have "no more than three internal development systems" (a bringing out of theology, associating, or disassociating).[73] The closure should then return to the idea of the opening statement. It should be "a terse, final sentence."[74]

In Buttrick's homiletic world, transitions are an unnecessary and artificial appendage. Well-written moves join together in natural conversational logic. The important thing is to state the move with conversational language and logic.[75]

The following series of moves lack connective logic:

We are all sinners.
We have been forgiven in Jesus Christ.
We can live in a new way.

They could be better written as follows:

Be honest: We are all sinners,
But we have been forgiven by Jesus Christ,
So we can now live new lives.[76]

The second example is written in conversational language and shows connective logic.

Buttrick sums up his theory of moves thus: "Moves must form as separate meanings with strong starts and strong conclusions. At the same time, moves must display a connecting logic obvious to a congregation. Structure must be sharply defined and sequence naturally logical."[77]

The second section of Buttrick's treatise is labeled *structures*. This has to do with the larger structure of a sermon: moves in connection. Buttrick identifies three basic modes of sermon construction: immediacy (perhaps parallel to narrative forms), reflection (a mode often used with epistles), and praxis (dealing with matters of practical importance). Each structure must be guided not by a central idea but by an intention—either an *intending of* or an *intending toward* (Buttrick's terminology, which is similar to the concept of homiletic purpose).

What is controversial about Buttrick's approach is his attempt to ground homiletics in contemporary rhetoric. Instead of employing the classic rhetoric of traditional homiletics, Buttrick employs a phenomenological approach to language. Phenomenology is a philosophy that says that reality consists of objects and events as they are perceived or understood in human consciousness. A phenomenological approach to language promotes ambiguity and makes much use of image, narrative, dialogue, metaphor, and symbol.[78] Using this approach, then, Buttrick builds his homiletic on scientific research (research which he fails to document in the book). Instead of beginning with theology and moving toward the preaching event, Buttrick begins with the listening process and moves toward theology.

What can we say about Buttrick's homiletic of moves? His strength is the clear description he offers of one way in which sermons can be formed. Rather than dealing in vague principles, Buttrick is willing to give very definite *rules*. The preacher who follows Buttrick's rules will find that they are an effective way to design and construct a sermon. Particularly helpful is his clear discussion of moves, their design, and their connection. Rather than the abstract ideas of many books on preaching, in Buttrick we find definite guidelines and examples.

Equally helpful is Buttrick's discussion of the process of sermon formation. Begin with a basic structure,[79] he instructs us, then develop an expanded sketch,[80] and then form a final structure.[81] His comments on the process of sermon development are insightful: "We are not trying to produce a finished sermon, one section at a time, . . . [rather] we are trying to 'flesh out,' in a rough way, the *whole* structure."[82]

But his strength is also his weakness. Buttrick's design for sermon form is not the only way sermons can be formed. Long asks, "Do ideas really get formed in human consciousness in the way Buttrick claims they do? They *can*, I suppose, but surely not in every case."[83] Many ideas come to us differently and are capable of being expressed differently than Buttrick demands. Buttrick offers one approach that can be helpful, but he must be read with care and discernment.

A Variety of Forms

So given the various shapes that sermons take, which form should be used? Haddon Robinson once made the bold statement: "There is no such thing as sermon form!" By that statement he meant, I think, that a variety of sermon forms are possible and no one form is right for every sermon. Sometimes a deductive form is just the thing. Often we will reach for an inductive or narrative structure. At times we may venture into the world of story preaching. There are many possibilities. Our preaching ministry should reflect the rich diversity of form that we discover in the Scriptures.

3

The Theology
of Design

Pastor Bill sits at his desk pondering his sermon. Sunday looms large on his horizon. Scattered across his desk are various books he has encountered on his journey into the world of homiletics. One book recommends a narrative form, another speaks of story sermons, a third talks of sermons designed to produce faith-consciousness. Still another contains a series of creative approaches to sermon structure. He wonders if perhaps his preaching would be better if he could break out of his homiletic rut into new and different forms of expression. Perhaps narrative, story, image, and inductive movement are the saviors that will rescue his sermons from the homiletic doldrums and bring them into the cutting edge of contemporary preaching.

Yet a nagging question remains: Are such approaches to preaching really biblical? Is it possible that the new improved forms for preaching are really just old and unbiblical compromises with contemporary culture? Could it be, he asks himself, that the truth of the gospel is somehow being sacrificed on the altar of relevance?

Pastor Bill is right to ask tough questions. Current homiletic approaches did not materialize in a vacuum. Their ascendancy to popularity did not just happen. Today at least three winds of influence swirl around contemporary homiletic discussion: theology, literary criticism, and culture. Pastors who would think deeply about the form of their sermons and who care about faithfulness to the gospel must wrestle with the issues raised by each of these areas of thought. In this chapter we will focus on the question of theology and sermon form. If we are to understand the roots of sermon design, we must engage sermon form theologically. Form is not just a matter of practice but of theology.

The Validity of Sermon Form

The first question that must be addressed in prelude to any investigation into sermon form is Does it really matter? In other words, should preachers care about sermon form? Is sermon structure really a valid concern? Thomas Long notes, "There has always been the nagging suspicion, surfacing from time to time, that it is unbecoming for the preacher . . . to be concerned in a significant way about the sermon's design."[1]

Some would make a case that form should flow so naturally from the content of the gospel that any discussion of design should be unnecessary. After all, they contend, the New Testament preachers and apostles did not concern themselves with questions of inductive or deductive design, introductions or conclusions. Neither should the preacher worry much about the structure of sermons. The preacher should just—well, preach. Like the baseball player who, overly concerned with the technicalities of his swing, becomes an ineffective hitter, the preacher who becomes too concerned with sermon design may lose vitality in preaching.

Karl Barth, in his volume *Homiletics*, states "There is no need, then, to consider the problem of what should come first, second, and third. The preacher has only to repeat what the text says."[2] Barth rejects introductions, conclusions, and sermon divisions out of his theological conviction that humanity can do nothing to make the Word of God effective and should not try to do so, perhaps because of his dislike for the artiness of the sermons of his day.[3] For Barth, sermon form only served to obscure the Word of God.[4] Preachers, he argued, need not make much of the issue of sermon form.

The problem with this line of reasoning is that the biblical preachers and writers did have a concern for design. Long argues that the New Testament writers were intentional in their rhetorical design and that New Testament preaching was based on the preaching of the synagogue, which was complex in its communication strategy.[5] Consider the difference between Paul's sermon in Acts 13 to a largely Jewish audience in the synagogue and his sermon in Acts 17 to a Gentile audience in the Greek marketplace. In Acts 13 Paul's sermon is filled with Old Testament references and theology. In Acts 17 Paul takes a very different approach, appealing to an altar to "an unknown God" and quoting from Greek poets, while not using a single quotation from the Hebrew Scriptures. These two sermons reflect different audiences and thus different rhetorical designs. They are designed differently, but they are designed.

Form is inescapable. Even if one simply reads the text, issues of design must be considered. Even Barth's sermons had introductions, conclusions, and structure.[6] H. Grady Davis comments that the difference between "chaotic thought and ordered thought is not the difference between no form and form; it is the difference between confused form and organized form . . . the only question is, what form?"[7]

Yet it is proper to raise concerns about the current focus on form. Issues of design and structure cannot be allowed to overshadow the content of the word to be spoken. The goal of the sermon can never be eloquence or aesthetics; the goal must always be to speak the gospel well. Sermonizing may be an art, but it is doubtful whether sermons are intended to be works of art.

Perhaps a balance can be found. Sermons must always be designed and thus must be concerned with issues of form. The preacher must always wrestle with questions of structure. And yet such matters must never be allowed to take precedence over the content of the gospel we preach. Indeed, form must always flow from content. Sermon form must be the servant of the text, not its master. It is right, then, once the preacher has done the work of exegesis and study and has a message to speak, to carefully consider the form of the sermon.

Theology

There remains a deeper concern: the suspicion that theological issues are tied up in this business of form. Perhaps form is more than an issue of practice. Maybe sermon design is also a matter of theology. If so, more may be at stake than mere effectiveness in homiletic delivery.

Preaching is a theological task. The preacher has the responsibility of taking God's truth and proclaiming that truth to the world. Preachers are schooled in theology and biblical studies. And the best preachers take pride in the time they invest in Bible study and theological thought. They pay attention to the theological nature of the homiletic mandate.

What has often been left out from preaching preparation is any serious theological reflection on the matter of form. Of course we use form—our sermons are structured. It is impossible to preach without form. But we often fail to recognize that there are theological questions related to the forms we choose. The discussion of form is often seen as a matter of pragmatics. We use the patterns we were taught in seminary, we take the form our tradition mandates, or we employ the style with which we feel most comfortable. The more innovative among us learn to use forms that relate well to modern culture. In essence, we use "what works." Pragmatism is our master.

What we need, however, is a renewed understanding of sermon form as a matter of theology. Sermonic form has its roots deep in the soil of theological discussion. As thoughtful preachers we must enter into that dialogue. Theology will affect the forms we use. And the forms we use will influence the theology we communicate. The relationship may at times seem muddy and the issues obscure, but theology is related to sermon structure.

What are the theological issues that intersect with sermon form? Let me call attention to four concerns.

Theology of Scripture Affects Sermon Structure

Simply put, the preacher who can confidently say, "Thus says the Lord!" will shape his sermons differently than those who are uncertain of the veracity of the Bible. Preachers who hold to the truthfulness of Scripture may use different forms than those who are less sure. Or at the very least, they will use those forms differently. Those who hold to an evangelical view of Scripture (a confidence in the authority and truthfulness of Scripture) will not shy away from proposition or direct address. They may make use of narrative and induction or even occasionally story forms, but always in the service of a biblical idea and biblical content. The sermon will both do something and say something. The sermon will consist of both image and proposition.

Conversely, those who question the truthfulness of Scripture may tend toward forms that are less direct. They may use story, narrative, and inductive structures exclusively. Their forms may be vague and open-ended. They will attempt to create an experience of the gospel, perhaps forgetting (or not admitting) that the sermon must also communicate propositional truth.

Some sermon forms may not be congenial to an evangelical view of Scripture. A sermon that is overly vague and open-ended does not keep good company with an inspired text. Long has suggested that the utterly open-ended sermon may be a betrayal of the gospel itself.[8]

Our theology of Scripture affects not only sermon content but sermon design as well. Our view of Scripture does (and certainly should) influence our sermon structure.

Ecclesiology Can Affect the Form of the Sermon

It is not just our view of Scripture that is interpreted through sermon form but our view of the church as well. Ecclesiology is one of the more promising areas of homiletical inquiry that also relates to the form of the sermon. In what way should our understanding of the church as the people of God affect sermon form? How does the rhetorical situation (preaching in the context of church) influence the design of the sermon?

Let us begin by noting that ecclesiology affects sermon design since we speak in the context of the church. All preaching is done in the context of the church. Although some preaching may occur "outside" of the church, all preaching speaks the church's stories, uses the church's language, and is part of the church's mandate. Acts 2 records that the believers in Jerusalem "devoted themselves to the apostles' teaching and to the fellowship, to the breaking of bread and to prayer" (v. 42). The text continues, describing how they met each other's needs, ate together, and praised God, and ends by adding that "the Lord added to their number daily those who were being saved" (v. 47). The church grew through the preaching of the apostles. How did such powerful preaching happen? It happened in the context and in the language of the church of God. According to Richard Lischer, "Preaching is not represented as one person's persuasive address. It is the ceaseless activity of the church."[9] Preaching of necessity reflects the character of the church. The church is always in view even if only in the background.

This issue comes into sharp focus in the debate over *seeker* sermons. The term *seeker* is commonly used to designate those who are open to the Christian faith but who have not yet made a commitment of faith. Preachers who see themselves as speaking primarily to seekers and to those who are new to the faith will form their sermons differently from those who understand themselves as speaking primarily to Christians. Rick Warren, pastor of Saddleback Valley Community Church, once stated that he uses different styles to preach to seekers than he uses to teach believers. Warren uses different structures in different situations because of the perceived context. Warren sees his preaching in seeker services as directed primarily to those outside the church. This explains why Warren and most seeker churches primarily make use of topical sermons on Sunday morning. The primary audience is the seeker, and topical sermons are viewed as being more relevant to those outside of the church or to those who are new to the Christian faith. The debate over "seeker" sermons is really a discussion of the relationship between the church and sermon form!

Our view of the church and the purpose for which the church gathers will affect how we design our sermons. Is the church primarily a teaching station? If so, we will design didactic teaching sermons. Is the church a place to bring unbelievers for hearing the gospel? Then we will likely create topical sermons using a subject-completed pattern. Is the church gathering primarily intended to reinforce our identity as the people of God? In that case we may make great use of narrative and story. All of this is to say that our view of the particular rhetorical situation and its relationship to the church will affect the forms we use.

These are some of the reasons why it is impossible to leave our view of the church out of the process of sermon design. Our view of the audience to whom we speak and their relationship to the church will help to form our sermons. When the preacher stands to speak, the history, language, heritage, and traditions of the church shape the words spoken. No preacher stands alone. We must always preach in the context of the church. Even the most radical seeker sermon cannot ignore the presence of the church (usually the majority of people in a seeker service are believers). The fact that believers are present is a rhetorical force that cannot be ignored. The sermon is part of an ongoing dialogue, and that dialogue will affect the sermon design. The rhetorical situation affects not only the content of what we preach but necessarily (given the relationship of substance and form) the structure of what we say. The sermon forms we use reflect, at least in part, our view of the church.

Anthropology Influences Sermon Form

Fred Craddock notes that it is "especially [the preacher's] doctrine of man" that can affect preaching design.[10] We must preach to people, and our understanding of the nature of humanity and of how people hear and respond will necessarily influence the form of our sermons. There is a close connection between homiletical form and anthropology.[11]

Every form reflects a view of humanity. Propositional forms reflect an emphasis on humanity's rationality. Narrative and story see the essence of humanity as living in narrative. Inductive preaching understands that people approach life in a certain (inductive) way. These views of humanity are not mutually exclusive. People are rational beings, they do live in narrative, and they naturally approach life in an inductive manner. But different forms will tend to emphasize one aspect over another.

Our view of humanity in sin will affect our form. If we understand people to be fallen and in need of salvation and inner transformation, we may choose forms that are more direct or capable of direct address. Some doctrines such as condemnation and the horror of hell demand a certain directness to our speech. Of course, even narrative and inductive forms, though more indirect, can be designed using direct address. Consider Nathan's narrative to David in 2 Samuel 12 and the direct address he employed ("You are the man!"). You cannot get much more direct than that.

If our view of humanity is more optimistic (and unbiblical, i.e., "people are basically good"), we may design sermons more for their aesthetic impact. The sermon form may be more vague, open-ended, and inconclusive. Our view of humanity affects our sermon form, and every sermon form reflects an anthropology.

Language Theory Can Affect Sermon Form

John McClure points out that theories of language (which ultimately is a hermeneutical and theological issue) also relate to homiletical decisions. He suggests that two major theories of language have impacted contemporary homiletics: empirical theories and phenomenological theories. Empirical theories of language hold that "the rules for language and for the creation of meaning are bound to behavior and to physical laws."[12] One of the effects of an empirical theory of language is a denotative style. "Preachers with denotative styles strive to achieve clarity of language and logic. They use clear, common language and are less inclined to use figurative language such as metaphor, image, or symbol. They prefer deductive forms of logic or forms that have cultural and communal precedents."[13] On the other hand, those who hold to phenomenological theories of language give the "priority to metaphor and symbol" in their preaching.[14] Preachers with a phenomenological understanding of language are more likely to adopt a connotative style.

Preachers with connotative styles use language and forms of logic that promote ambiguity and subtlety in communication.

They use image, narrative, dialogue, metaphor, and symbol to keep hearers on the hook and in pursuit of ideas or meaning. Narrative, inductive, and conversational homiletical theories promote connotative styles.[15] David Buttrick includes a chapter on language in his book *Homiletic*. He tells us, "The language of preaching is a connotative language used with theological precision."[16] He stresses metaphor, symbol, and mystery.

Although it is beyond the scope of this book to decide the foundational issues involved in linguistic studies, it is important for the preacher to recognize the influence that the philosophy of language has on sermon form.

Sermon form, then, is not just a matter of what works. It involves significant theological issues that relate to the forms we use. Bryan Chapell reminds us that "preachers must learn the value of many types of communication, but appropriate usage requires us to understand the underpinnings of each."[17] We may not be able to resolve all the issues, but understanding what the issues are is important. The discerning preacher is aware of these theological concerns as he structures his sermons.

Theology of Preaching and Sermon Form

Another issue that thoughtful preachers must consider is the theology of preaching itself. Closely related to the issue of theology is the question of just what a sermon is to do. There is an interrelationship between theology proper, one's theology of preaching, and sermon form.

The theology of preaching, or what a sermon is to accomplish, affects the forms we choose to use. Purpose in preaching cannot help but be related to the structure of our sermons. When the purpose is informational, certain forms will be used; when the purpose is to create an impression or cause something to happen in the life of the listener, then other forms may be chosen.

In traditional homiletics the purpose of a sermon was to bring an idea or concept across the homiletical bridge, which connected the text with the listener. Traditional forms served this purpose well. The sermon was intended to convey an idea, which would be written as a proposition. This approach parallels what George

Lindbeck has labeled the "cognitive model" of doctrine,[18] which stresses the objectivity of doctrinal truth claims.

But more recently the emphasis has been on the sermon as an event or experience. It is more a feeling, an emotion, or an event that is to be brought across the bridge. The focus is more on what should happen in the sermon rather than on informational content. This parallels what Lindbeck calls "the experiential-expressive model" of doctrine. This model focuses on "non-informative and non-discursive symbols of inner feelings, attitudes, and existential orientations."[19] This view of doctrine is reflected in David Randolph's definition of preaching as "the *event* in which the biblical text is interpreted in order that its meaning will come to expression in the concrete situation of the hearers."[20] The sermon, then, is often seen primarily as an *event*. Many homileticians have rightly noted that a sermon is far more than the transfer of information (e.g., "The Greek word here means . . ."). The sermon is not static but dynamic; something should happen during the preaching time. We are to preach the text, not just about the text. It is in this theological soil that narrative, storytelling, and other more innovative forms have taken the deepest root. Sometimes in this approach the fact that the Bible does *say* quite a bit (i.e., contains propositional truth) is overlooked.

The preacher's approach to preaching in terms of function is directly related to sermon form. When it was thought that a proposition must be communicated, a rational, discursive form predominated. Didache reigned. But if feelings and attitudes are what need to be communicated, nondirect, inductive preaching may be best.

Those who advocate an experiential-expressive approach to preaching will probably gravitate toward a narrative or story form of preaching as the most effective means of communicating on this level. Some have recommended that these forms be used exclusively.

But it is not necessary to choose between cognitive and expressive models for homiletics, because sermons communicate on more than one level. Both ideas and feelings and attitudes can be part of the sermon purpose. Sermons are both conceptual and eventful. As Long points out, "Biblical texts say things that do things, and the sermon is to say and do those things too."[21] A sermon should have both a focus and a function (to use Long's language) or an idea and a purpose (as Haddon Robinson puts it[22]).

If we understand sermons as both word and event, then some sermon forms may not be appropriate (at least on a regular basis). Sermon forms that are overly vague, ambiguous, and open-ended may be rejected as not communicating the idea of the text, while strict arguments or the exclusive use of propositional forms may fail to do justice to what the sermon intends to do.

Yet a variety of sermon forms are possible. At times a narrative sermon will work, at other times a more didactic approach will be best. Our approach to sermon form should be as varied as the Bible's own approach to genre. The intention of the text and the intention of the sermon will govern the choice of sermon form.

The Implications of Theology for Sermon Form

What, then, are the implications of theology for the design of Sunday's sermon? What conclusions do we come to? Though the results are at times obscure, some broad issues emerge.

The concern for form is unavoidable. Sermons must be designed, and preachers must ask questions about the forms their sermons take. Although the content of the sermon must be given priority, the preacher will not be unconcerned with structure. It will not do to say, "This is the form I learned in seminary." The preacher must ask, "Which form most faithfully communicates the theology of this text?"

Second, form is not theologically neutral. The message is not just what is said but also how it is said. An essential interrelationship exists between content and structure, message and medium. Sermon form is a theological issue.

Some forms may be judged inappropriate on theological grounds. Sermon forms that are overly ambiguous and open-ended may not be compatible with the belief that God has spoken to us with clarity. And a consistent diet of purely discursive sermons may not do justice to the intent of the Scripture.

A variety of forms can be used. Inductive forms can be used that do not avoid direct address. Narrative sermons can make propositional claims. Deductive sermons can be sensitive to the way people listen. Our sermon form, then, should reflect our theology in general, the theology of the particular text, and our theology of preaching.

Perhaps Pastor Bill is still confused about how all this relates to this Sunday's sermon—but he now understands that form is very much a theological matter. He must choose his form with care. He now turns his attention to a second consideration: the relationship between the literary form and the sermon form.

4

LITERARY CONCERNS AND SERMON FORM

Pastor Bill is perched on the horns of a homiletic dilemma. He now knows there are various sermon forms available for his use for Sunday's sermon. He could choose a narrative form or perhaps go with a more deductive approach. But he wonders which form for this sermon? Why choose narrative over deductive for this week's message? He turns to a chapter in a new book on preaching that just came from Amazon.com. The first sentence reads: "Literary genre should influence the form of the sermon." His appetite whetted, he reads on . . .

In December 2005, C. S. Lewis's rich Christian allegory of redemption, *The Lion, The Witch and the Wardrobe*, released as a movie. Imagine that instead of appearing in story form, as Lewis wrote his work of fiction, the movie was produced as a documentary, complete with interviews from literary scholars and theologians. The movie would probably define terms and explain the meaning of various images found in the book. "Aslan," it could be stated, "represents Jesus Christ." In addition to being tedious to watch and almost certainly a financial disaster, such an attempt would not be a faithful interpretation of the original work, because the literary form, allegorical story, is part of the meaning of Lewis's work. The documentary might get at some of the meaning, but it would lose much of the emotional impact. To be faithful to Lewis's book, the movie had to be produced as story.

Something similar happens when we move into the arena of preaching. Scripture comes to us with literary forms, and those forms are part of the meaning. If we are to be faithful to the Scripture, we must consider the literary forms of the Bible. When we design our sermons, we must ask, How can the form of the text have some effect on the form of the sermon?

In the world of public address, preaching is somewhat unusual. Most public speaking is communication that finds its authority and content from a variety of sources. But preaching finds both its authority and its (primary) content in a single text, the Bible. In preaching we are attempting not only to make a speech but to communicate the meaning of a biblical text. There is a relationship between text and sermon. And that relationship goes beyond the relationship of textual content to sermon content. It also embraces the relationship between literary and sermonic form. In this chapter, we want to explore two ways in which the literary forms of the Bible can influence sermon form: the form of the various genres of the text and the shape of biblical sermons.

The Relationship between the Form of the Text and the Form of the Sermon

The Bible comes to us with form. There are hills and valleys and plains in the landscape of Scripture. The Word of God comes to us in various genres or forms. A genre can be defined as a group of written texts that evidence distinctive and recurring characteristics.[1] And although there is general agreement today on the importance of genre, there is no consensus on the number or identity of the genres of the Bible. In any case, some of the major genres include narrative, prophecy, wisdom, psalm, gospel, epistle, and apocalypse.[2] Beyond the major genre categories are forms that can be understood as subsets of the major genres. These include miracle, law, parable, lament, exhortation, autobiography, and lawsuit.[3] Each of these forms or genres helps to shape the meaning and purpose of the texts in which it is found.

One of the important insights in recent homiletical thought has been the relationship between the genre of the text and the form of the sermon. Scholars have discovered a significant truth, which we have already alluded to: the form of the text is part of the meaning of the text, and thus there ought to be a relationship between that form and sermon form. We must decide "how to preach so that the sermon embodies in its language, form, and style the gospel it seeks to proclaim."[4] The literary form of the text ought to bear a significant relationship to sermon shape. So literary form cannot be left behind at the conclusion of the exegetical process; it must somehow wander into the sermon.

This homiletical concern began first in the field of literary criticism. The focus of attention in literary criticism has shifted from the historical questions of the nineteenth century to the text and its forms and the relationship that exists between text and form. Amos Wilder demonstrated the essential connection between form and content. Wilder does this by showing the interconnection between form and substance in art, artifacts (he mentions the axe and the airplane), and literature. As one cannot separate the shape and substance of a work of art, neither should we separate form and significance in literature. "Shape and substance are inseparable and mutually determinative,"[5] Wilder concludes. What the Bible says and how it says it must not be separated. There is then a relationship between content and form.

Traditional homiletics paid scant attention to genre. The procedure usually followed was to exegete the passage, identify the central idea, and then discard the form. What was brought across the homiletical bridge was a preachable idea—the literary form was left behind.

More recently, however, there has been a firestorm of renewed appreciation for the integral relationship between textual form and sermon form. Homileticians, building on the work of literary criticism, have suggested that the form of a text ought to influence the form of the sermon. A sermon on a narrative text ought to be structured differently than a sermon on a proverb. The form of a sermon on an apocalyptic text ought to be different from the form of a sermon on a parable. Why should the gospel "always be impaled upon the frame of Aristotelian logic," asks Fred Craddock, "when [the preacher's] muscles twitch and his nerves tingle to mount the pulpit not with three points but with the gospel as narrative or parable or poem or myth or song?"[6]

Some have gone almost so far as to suggest that the form of the text determines the form of the sermon. John Holbert says that "the best expression of a narrative is a narrative."[7] Henry Mitchell suggests that to use a different form than the one inherent in the text is to do violence to the meaning of the text.[8] Of course, such a position is easier to maintain with some forms than with others, and probably no one would seek to apply it absolutely.

A Relationship of Influence

Most homileticians have recognized that the relationship between literary form and sermon form must be less direct than some have suggested. They have noticed that text and sermon are different types of communication (literary vs. oral/aural), have different audiences and different cultural contexts, and often have different purposes. Therefore one cannot simply take the form of the text as the form of the sermon. Craddock, in *Preaching*, notes that sermon shape does not have to come from the form of the text: "A text that is a prayer does not necessitate a sermon in prayer form."[9]

A better approach is to allow the textual form to influence the shape of the sermon. Sidney Greidanus says that the sermon form reshapes the form of the text.[10] The goal of sermon form then is "respect for the text."[11] Somehow we want to bring something of the literary form over into the sermon.

Thomas Long's book entitled *Preaching and the Literary Forms of the Bible* exemplifies Greidanus's approach. Long asks five questions: (1) What is the genre of the text? (2) What is the rhetorical function of this genre? (3) What literary devices does this genre employ to achieve its rhetorical effect? (4) How in particular does the text under consideration, in its own literary setting, embody the characteristics and dynamics described in questions 1–3? And (5) How may the sermon, in a new setting, say and do what the text says and does in its setting?[12] In this approach the textual form is allowed to influence the form of the sermon. The sermon form recreates the textual form in some way. The focus is perhaps more on the rhetorical function of the form than it is on the form itself.

What do we learn from the renewed interest in genre? We need to allow the rhetorical function of the text to have some say in the formation of the sermon. This means that we must pay attention to genre and its function in a particular passage. At times this may mean employing the same form as the text. Narrative is the most obvious example. A narrative text will most often call for a narrative sermon. But at times the impact of the form of the text will be more subtle. We may try to interweave the imagery and tone of a psalm into the fabric of our sermon or make use of the symbolism of apocalyptic throughout a sermon on a text from Revelation. Or we could make the single point of a parable[13] the single point of our sermon.

A Relationship of Variety

The current interest in literary form also reminds us that if God has used a variety of forms to communicate his message, then the preacher would do well to use a variety of forms to communicate that same message today. Scripture abounds with a diversity of literary forms. Why should our sermons use only one didactic design? Or even one narrative design? Story, narrative, poetry, and other more reflective as well as more didactic

approaches all cry out to be put to use in the proclamation of
the good news.

We must take care that whatever approach we take toward
structure should be flexible and varied enough to reflect the
varied forms of the Bible. What preacher has not noticed that
the Bible was not written with sections containing three parallel
points? Rather the logic of Scripture twists and turns, showing
cause and effect at one point, digressing at another, pausing to
linger over a powerful image, then meeting objections raised by
an unknown questioner. The structure of Scripture is more often
inductive than deductive. Our approach to sermon structure must
be able to reflect the varied structures of Scripture.

Here are some examples of how genre can influence the form
of the sermon. The first is from a narrative portion in the Gospels.
I structured a sermon on the prodigal son from Luke 15:11–32
as follows:

1. There were two sons. The younger one was looking for his
   freedom.
2. But freedom isn't all it's cracked up to be. He ran into
   problems.
3. Well, then he comes to his senses. We call it repentance.
   He headed home to admit his sin.
4. But even before he got there—his father was waiting, ready
   to celebrate. "Let's have a party," cries the dad.
5. But there was a dissenting voice in all this joy—the older
   brother.

Such a structure is more a plot than an outline. It makes use
of the language of story and follows the contours of the story in
Luke 15. The plot of the sermon came from the plot of Jesus's
story. It attempts to carry across the homiletical bridge not only
the theological content of the text (God's love and compassion
for sinners) but something of the form of the text as well.

A second example comes from Paul's Epistle to the Philippians.
The text is Philippians 1:9–11. I delivered this sermon at my son's
wedding. The form of the text is a prayer. So I wrote the sermon
as a prayer. Each of the main points was written: "My prayer for
you is . . ." And then I concluded the sermon by praying for them.
The form of the sermon reflected the form of the text.

Of course it is not always so easy to see how the form of the text can influence the form of the sermon. But in preparing for each sermon, some attempt should be made to identify a way or ways in which the form of the text can influence the form of the sermon. By doing so, we respect the form of the text.

The Relationship between the Sermons of the Bible and Sermon Form

A second area of literary form, which has implications for sermon design, is the structure of Bible sermons. But the Bible has no sermons, we are told. "Clearly," says O. C. Edwards Jr., "there is little in the New Testament that can be identified . . . as Christian Preaching."[14] True enough, if by "sermons" what is meant is verbatim sermons in their entirety. But the Bible does contain recorded speech acts, which could well be classified as condensed versions of sermons. The sermons of Jesus and the speeches of Acts, while perhaps not composed of the *ipsissima verba* of Jesus or the apostles, does recall the *ipsissima vox*.[15] The speeches of Acts can be understood as summaries of longer addresses. Even the Epistles, which were intended to be read in the churches, had a homiletical/sermonic function.[16] The preaching in the Bible is a faithful reflection of actual sermons and thus is available to us for rhetorical analysis.

The Preaching of Jesus

Jesus is portrayed in the Gospels as preaching in a variety of different circumstances. His preaching varies from the clear proclamation of the kingdom of God to the enigma of the parables. Jesus does not shy away from direct address: "Repent, for the kingdom of heaven is near" (Matt. 4:17). Yet he is often very indirect. The parables are frequently cited as the best example of indirect preaching. "Like inductive preaching the parables begin with the concrete particulars of human life, move like a story, invite the participation of the hearers and require the hearers to draw their own conclusions," says Charles Campbell.[17] A significant difference between most contemporary preaching and the parables of Jesus is the rhetorical situation. The parables are mostly out-of-church preaching, at times intended to conceal as much as to reveal, while most Christian preaching is in-church preaching. Yet one thing is clear—Jesus used a wide diversity of styles and forms in proclaiming his message. Jesus was creative in his preaching.

If we are to follow in Jesus's footsteps, if we are to preach like Jesus, we will make use of a variety of forms. We will make use of story and induction. But we will also use the language of direct address when appropriate.

The Preaching of the Apostles

The best we can do to investigate the preaching of the apostles is to turn to the book of Acts. Acts contains a number of speeches from the apostles and their representatives. Luke, the author of Acts, probably played a role in editing and shaping the speeches, but the speeches had their origin with the apostles and, in the case of Acts 7, with Stephen. Though most of the speeches in Acts follow the general pattern of prophecy and fulfillment, some are radically different.

In Acts 7, Stephen tells the whole story of Israel's rejection of God's representatives before getting to his point, the rejection of Jesus in verse 52. Stephen was preaching to what proved to be a hostile audience (stoning the speaker to death is always classified as a hostile response!). He withheld the full idea of his message (that Jesus Christ was the Messiah) until the end of the speech. If he hadn't delayed the central idea of his message, it would most certainly have been a much shorter sermon since his listeners would not have allowed him to conclude it. His preaching was inductive/narrative in form.

In Acts 13 Paul is speaking to a mixed audience (Jew and Gentile). He uses a primarily deductive form. There is a brief inductive beginning leading up to the introduction of Jesus as Savior (vv. 16–23). The remainder of the sermon explains, proves, and applies that truth in deductive fashion.

Paul in Athens (Acts 17), preaching to a primarily Gentile audience, uses a very inductive form of proclamation. He was attempting to communicate to a people who were highly influenced by pagan philosophy and largely unaware of Jewish history or the Hebrew Scriptures, and who could not be expected to be receptive to the idea of the resurrection.

Paul instinctively understood that he could not begin with
Jesus or the Scriptures or the resurrection. Instead he takes his
starting point from an altar to an unknown God. Along the way
he quotes from two Greek poets. Finally, he concludes with a call
to repentance and the startling revelation of the resurrection of
Jesus. This sermon is perhaps the best precursor we have to the
modern "seeker" sermons.

In Paul's message to the Ephesian elders in Acts 20, he begins
inductively with his own story. He first describes some of the
characteristics of his ministry (vv. 18–21), then moves to his
journey toward Jerusalem (vv. 22–24), and finally arrives at a
most stunning revelation: Paul, who had fully proclaimed the
will of God to them, would no longer be with them (vv. 25–27).
From that point on in his message Paul moves more deductively
to the implications of that conclusion for his listeners. Because
Paul would not be there they must keep watch over the flock
(vv. 28–31). Because Paul would not be there they must depend
fully on the grace of God that was exemplified in Paul's ministry
(vv. 32–35). Paul uses both inductive and deductive movement
in his rhetorical strategy for delivering this message.

Don Sunukjian points out that the structure of Paul's sermon
in Acts 13 is deductive, his sermon in Acts 17 is mostly inductive,
and his sermon in Acts 20 is both inductive and deductive.[18] Paul
employed a diversity of rhetorical designs in his preaching.

No, we do not have any sermon manuscripts in the New Testament. But we do have considerable evidence for a variety in
sermon form both in the preaching of Jesus and of the apostles.
Not only are the genres of Scripture varied, but the sermons of
the Scriptures show a great deal of variety in the forms available and used.

Three Concluding Implications

Both the variety of genre in the Bible and the variety of forms
found in the sermons and speeches in the Bible teach us something about how we should shape sermons. Three implications
can be noted.

First, there is no such thing as the right sermon form. Various
forms are available for our use. Like a carpenter with a box full

of tools, the preacher has many designs available. Whatever form best conveys the meaning of the text to one's audience is the right form for that particular sermon.

Second, the preacher should intentionally seek to use a variety of sermon forms. It is easy to get in structural ruts. Preachers tend, if they are not careful, to design sermons in similar ways. I have learned that I tend to get in inductive ruts—but it is still a rut! Yet I have also learned that I can, with some effort, incorporate greater variety in the design of my sermons. I can, from time to time, employ more deductive teaching forms. We learn from the literary forms of the Bible and the forms of Bible preaching that every preacher should seek for variety not only in content but also in form.

I noticed a skyscraper in a big city recently. It soared into the sky with sweeping lines. It was refreshing because of its unique architectural design. If all buildings in that city were designed just like that one, the cityscape would become boring. This particular building was interesting because it was different. Of course, not every sermon design can be unique, but the more we pursue variety in form and the connection between literary form and sermon form, the more refreshing our sermons may become.

Finally, as much as possible, our sermons should be influenced by the literary form of the text. If the form is part of the meaning, we should do our best to bring that meaning across the homiletical bridge. Some time should always be budgeted for considering how the form of the text can influence the form of the sermon. The path may not always be clear, but it is important to wrestle with the issue for a while. We must ask, How can the form of this text influence the form of my sermon?

Culture and Sermon Form

That narrative sermon on Sunday certainly went well, Pastor Bill thinks to himself as he steps into his study on Tuesday morning. He hesitates for a moment before stepping through the doorway as he notices two notes on the floor, which had been slid under his study door. He opens the first. It is from Doris, one of the senior citizens of the church. "Thank you for that wonderful sermon," she gushes. Pastor Bill feels his spirits rise. He had always thought that Doris was perceptive! He reads the note twice before finally reaching for the second. The second note has a different tone. "How about more of the Word, Pastor!!!" it shouts. "We need more than just stories." This note, of course, is unsigned.

Now Pastor Bill doesn't know how to feel. He is tempted to totally disregard the second note (after all, it was anonymous) and to maybe pin the first one onto his bulletin board. But wait a minute, he says to himself. Maybe there is something to be learned from both . . .

Some time ago I was invited to speak at an after-school event at my youngest daughter Sarah's public high school. It was a very diverse group, culturally and religiously. Many were there simply for the chance to win a raffle at the end. Some I knew would be sympathetic to my message. But others, I was just as sure, would be antagonistic. I knew I had to give careful attention not only to what I said but also to how I said it. As best I could, I needed to craft my talk in a way that would help them listen. That, again, is the question of form. Audience matters in the process of sermon design.

Audience, which is just another way of saying culture, should affect sermon design. Preaching is not a one-way street. Done well, it involves give-and-take between the preacher and the audience. The discerning pastor exegetes not only the text but the audience as well. Our understanding of the audience to whom we speak ought to affect the way we design sermons.

Sermon form is influenced not only from within the text, through theological and literary concerns, but also from without, through what can be labeled cultural concerns. Preaching is not done in a vacuum. The preacher must ask, What form will best communicate this idea and this purpose to this audience? The listener must be given a seat in the pastor's study and be allowed to participate in sermon design. The preacher must always be concerned with the listener.

How do we get at the question of audience and sermon form? We can start by studying the general culture in which we live and minister. There are certain distinctives that characterize modern culture or at least portions of modern culture. We speak today of Baby Boomers and Gen-Xers, moderns and postmoderns. The wise pastor takes time to learn something about each of these groups. We need to do our best to understand the shifting world in which we live. Audience can be understood in terms of these broad sociological categories.

But audience can also be considered more narrowly as the specific audience at the church on First and Main, rather than to everybody in general (or nobody in particular). Every pastor speaks to a particular audience, which is different from every other audience. So we want to consider our audience from these two perspectives: culture in general and the particular audience to whom we speak.

Culture and Sermon Form

No preacher can ignore the effects of culture. Preachers must not only be students of Scripture but also of the culture in which they live. Sermons are different today than they were a generation ago. To a large extent that is a reflection of changes in the culture. The Scriptures must have the priority in our sermon designing, but culture has a role to play.

Much of the impetus for new sermon forms finds its source in culture. We need new and fresh forms, we are told, because people hear differently today. Any reading of current society must grapple with the reality that though the heart of humanity has remained the same, the lifestyle and worldview of our day has changed significantly from the lifestyle and worldview of even a generation ago. We live in a different world. A paradigm shift has occurred. We now live in a time that is often labeled postmodern. A major impetus for Fred Craddock's book *As One without Authority* was the "radically changed situation" of his day.[1] It is not unreasonable to suggest that the situation is even more radically different today than it was in the 1970s when *As One without Authority* first released.

But caution must be exercised: the discontinuity between the "modern" era and the "postmodern" is not absolute. Similarities are greater than dissimilarities.[2] People are still people.

Yet there are significant cultural shifts. D. A. Carson lists several changes: an epistemological shift in our approach to truth; a decline in absolutism and an increase in perspectivalism (the idea that claims to truth are mostly a matter of point of view); a decrease in confidence in reason and our ability to know objective reality; and a corresponding emphasis on relationships, affective responses, and the importance of community and tradition.[3] These shifts have an impact on preaching and preaching form.

In *Marketplace Preaching*, Calvin Miller recalls us to preaching that engages culture. He tells us "to get outside the walls and find out once again what people are talking about and what their interests and needs really are."[4] This leads Miller to an emphasis on inductive preaching. He goes so far as to say that induction is *the* means of preaching.[5] Miller is right that listening to our culture should cause us to preach differently.

The different generations can be labeled Pre-Boomers (born 1927–1945), Boomers (born 1946–1964), Generation X (born 1965–1981) and Millennials (born since 1981).[6] Pre-Boomers and Boomers were born into modernity. They emphasize rationality and quality. The emphasis on excellence during the 1980s was really a Boomer characteristic. Generation X was born into modernity but has been deeply affected by postmodernity. Millennials were born into and raised in a postmodern world.

Baby Boomers

In *A Generation of Seekers*, Wade Clark Roof lists five defining factors that have shaped the lives of the Boomer generation: (1) the upheaval of the times (as epitomized particularly in the assassination of John Kennedy), (2) affluence (Boomers are a generation with high expectations and a sense of entitlement), (3) the gender revolution ("Boomers as a generation would have to deal with an enormous array of gender and lifestyle changes, affecting the lives of both men and women"[7]), (4) higher education (generating "new and more secular meaning systems competing with theistic interpretations of the nature of reality"[8]), and (5) the media.[9]

Of the five factors, the media has generated the greatest influence on sermon structure. By age sixteen the average Baby Boomer had watched between twelve thousand and fifteen thousand hours of television.[10] Television became their major source of information and, perhaps more than anything else, has shaped their sense of reality.[11] "Perhaps the most important impact of television was that it replaced the word with the image: Henceforth the dominant medium would be the fleeting, discontinuous flow of electromagnetic pictures."[12] There seems to be a general agreement that the advent of television (and other electronic media) has changed the way people listen. The short attention span of audiences accustomed to the quick images of television is one consequence of television's dominance. This is important for the overall length of sermons as well as for the length of each major sermon segment.

ORAL FORM

A primary change brought about by the electronic media is a return to orality. Walter Ong divides culture into three distinct stages: the oral or oral/aural; the script; and the electronic.[13] Ong explains that the electronic age is a period of secondary orality comparable to the primary orality of Old Testament times.[14] "The new age into which we have entered has stepped up the oral and aural."[15] Literate cultures are "characterized by objective, analytical, formal, logical communication" while oral cultures are marked by "subjective, informal and narrative forms of communication evident especially in personal and collective storytelling."[16] Since secondary orality includes both print and oral approaches to communication, it engages both the right and left brain.[17] It has similarities to both the oral/aural age as well as to the literary age of script. Perhaps computer communication is a good example of this: Internet communication includes graphics, video, and audio clips as well as the more literary communication of email.

This shift toward a secondary orality is significant. An oral age communicates differently than a literary age. Michael Quicke lists some of the changes involved in the move from a literate society to a society of secondary orality. This shift involves a move from simply idea to idea and story. It involves a change from impersonal, passive language to self-consciously informal language.[18] And it involves a shift from individuality to a sense of community. Barbara Bate remarks that in the world of orality, "worshipers tend to retain concrete sensory images and well-told stories rather than long trains of reasoning or complex theoretical language."[19] So imagery and story are important in an oral age.

This move toward orality will require changes in sermon form. Kathleen Hall Jamieson finds that one of the qualities that made Ronald Reagan so effective in the age of television was his ability to make use of narrative.[20] Story is particularly important for an oral culture. Inductive strategies will receive a better hearing in an oral world. The forms of preaching are altered by the electronic age.

There is a sense in which every culture is an oral culture. Preaching, after all, has always been an oral event. But there has been a significant move toward orality that began with the Boomer generation and has continued with the postmodern generations of today.

PARTICIPATION

Marshall McLuhan is well known in the world of media for introducing the concepts of hot and cool mediums. A medium that calls for multisense involvement and participation is labeled cool. A hot medium, on the other hand, excludes involvement and participation, and usually involves only a single sense. Television is a cool medium. McLuhan argues that television is a high participation event: "Television demands participation and involvement in depth of the whole being. It will not work as a background. It engages you."[21] This suggests that the television generation needs a higher degree of participation.

I have personally experienced this when visiting people in their homes. Occasionally, people will leave the television on while I am with them. When that happens I find it is very difficult to focus on the person with whom I am visiting. I am constantly drawn into the television story. It doesn't work as background, at least not for me. Similarly, effective preaching in a television age will require participation by the listener. Preaching forms that do not engage the listener in the dialogue of thought will not be effective.

It is precisely for this reason that Craddock in 1971 argued for the inductive approach to preaching. Inductive preaching, he said, involves the listener to a greater extent and is more suitable for the modern listener.[22] Inductive movement calls the hearer to participate in the sermon event. The same is true of narrative and story. Who does not like a good story? Listening to a story requires involvement. The listener must participate.

INTIMACY

"Instancy and intimacy would be the distinguishing features of [the electronic] media," according to Roof.[23] Quentin Schultz notes that television creates intimacy through close-up shots.[24] There has been a shift away from the style of oratory toward a more conversational form and approach to communication. Jamieson claims that Franklin Delano Roosevelt, with his fireside chats, was the first public figure to recognize and act on this shift.[25] How do we create intimacy in preaching? A conversational and oral style combined with narrative and story imagery will work to create a sense of intimacy in the preaching event. Other issues such as architecture (churches today tend to be built in the round instead of the long rectangular structures of a few generations ago), furniture (do we use a pulpit and if so how large a pulpit?), dress (formal or informal), and eye contact are also important in creating intimacy in preaching.

Postmoderns

Generation X and the Millennials are products of postmodernity. Indeed the world we live in today is largely a postmodern world. If we are to be effective in our preaching, we must know how to communicate to postmodern people. Postmodernity is characterized by epistemological uncertainty and moral relativism. This is the "whatever" generation. Quicke explains that there is a consensus that "postmodern people yearn for experience; authenticity; genuine relationships; holism in worship and life; mystery, wonder and awe in personal spirituality; and local stories that help make sense of their own stories."[26] Obviously there is much that is good in these postmodern yearnings.

How do we preach to this new generation? We will make use of dialogue, image, story, and narration. We keep them involved by using inductive structures. We cultivate a conversational and informal style. We convince them of the truth not just through proclaiming it as true but by telling stories that show it is true. Perhaps we have someone share her story as part of the sermon. We make much use of imagery (both verbal imagery and visual). Graham Johnston says that in preaching to the postmodern world we need to use a dialogical approach, inductive preaching, storytelling, drama, art, and audiovisuals.[27]

Dangers

There are, of course, dangers in overemphasizing culture. One such danger is the tendency to allow the needs of the culture to overwhelm the concerns of Scripture. The Bible can often be used simply as a textbook of answers for addressing felt needs.

When culture is given too large a role in the sermon process, there can be a temptation to do "whatever works" without much serious theological reflection. Too much attention to the culture can cause us to use forms that engage but which may not communicate the great truth of the Bible. We may be tempted to think that communication technique rather than the Word of God can transform lives. Too much emphasis on culture can lead to the precipice of cultural compromise.

But the courageous pastor will live with the tension: we must speak the Word of God, but we must speak it to the world in which we live. To the extent that it is possible and biblically and theologically faithful, the wise preacher will seek to use sermon forms that communicate well to today's world. We will use structures that flow first from the shape of the gospel and second from the way people listen.

The Church at First and Main

The study of culture can inform us about communication to our world in a general way. But at 11 o'clock on Sunday morning we don't speak to culture in general. We speak to a specific audience at a particular address. We need to know that audience.

Of course, pastors do know their audience. They know them through the normal give-and-take of church life and pastoral ministry. Pastors visit in the hospital; they are there in times of crisis and struggle. They know the young couple with marital problems, the executive who has just been "force adjusted" (i.e., laid off), and the widow who is still grieving the loss of her husband. Pastors know their people.

And yet it is possible to invite the listener into a more significant role in the design of our sermons. We can be more intentional in allowing our listeners a part in the sermon process.

Audience Analysis

All pastors should take some time to analyze their audiences. What percentage of a pastor's audience would be considered Boomers? How many are from Generation X? How many are Millennials? Is there a significant college presence? What is the average education of the listener? How many are men and how many women? How many are part of a minority group? What percentage of people on a Sunday morning are not yet believers? That kind of information can affect many aspects of the sermon including the sermon form. If there are a large percentage of young adults (age thirty or below) in attendance, you may want to make more use of narrative or inductive forms. Story and image in preaching will be important. The use of PowerPoint and visual images in the sermon may be valuable for some audiences. Take time to analyze your audience.

Life Situation Grid

You can include your audience in sermon preparation through what Don Sunukjian calls a life situation grid.[28] Across the top, label columns for men, women, marrieds, singles, and single again. On the side of the grid create rows for different age groups, college students, different professions, etc. After you have studied your text and developed your central idea, look for two to four intersections and ask how this sermon can be designed to speak to their specific needs. This has the benefit of keeping you from becoming too abstract. It will help you to understand the path your people walk. And it may help you find the way to your sermon form.

	Men	Women	Marrieds	Singles	Single again
Children					
Youth Seniors					
College Students					
Non-professional					
Professional					
Etc.					

Sermon Discussion

Another way to involve your congregation in the sermon process is through a sermon discussion. Each year I invite a group

of people to a sermon roundtable. We talk about the sermons of
the previous year. We talk about the strengths and weaknesses
of my preaching ministry. We discuss possible sermon ideas for
the coming year. Yes, it is a humbling experience! It is tough on
the ego. But it is also a helpful experience. I usually leave with a
few ideas for sermons for the coming year and some insights into
how I can do a better job at the task of preaching. The feedback
I receive has implications not only for sermon content but also
for sermon design.

Sermon Preparation as a Team

I have found it very helpful to take a team approach to sermon preparation as much as possible. My wife is an informal
member of my team. She reads my sermons each week before I
preach them and often has helpful suggestions. I also do sermon
planning with our leadership. Our leadership team consists of
our elders (two pastors and three lay elders). They bring different perspectives and they are in touch with different needs
and concerns within the congregation of which I am not always
aware. I usually leave these meetings with a greater sense of
confidence about what to preach (sermon content) and how to
preach it (sermon form).

Allowing the Audience to Influence Our Form

What do we learn from this quick survey of culture? First, we
take our beginning from the Bible itself. We do not allow culture
itself to be our starting place. Form should flow from the content
of the text and the form of the text. We begin with the shape of
the gospel in a particular text.

That, however, does not mean we cannot learn from and be
informed by the study of culture in general and of our own church
culture in particular. We will listen to the Word and we will listen to
our world. We will be concerned with the concerns of our people.
We will become listeners. I have heard of pastors who take their
laptops and do some of their sermon preparation at Starbucks. As
they observe people come and go and perhaps catch fragments of
conversation, it helps them get a handle on their world.

Preachers stand between two worlds: the world of the Bible and theology and the world to which they would communicate. One way to deal with this tension is to focus on only one world. So, one preacher focuses primarily, if not solely, on the Bible and faithfulness to the text. But another, more sensitive to the world around us, focuses on relevant communication. When we focus on only one world, the tension disappears.

But a better approach is to live with the tension. Exegete the text, but also exegete the audience.[29] Be concerned with content, but also with the *how* of presentation. And always be aware of the danger that the *how* does not corrupt the *what*. Careful preachers will care about both worlds. They will listen to the Scripture and will listen to the world in which they live. They will do their best to communicate the unchanging truth of God to an ever-changing world.

6

An Evangelical
Approach

"Pastor, it seems to me that your preaching has been kind of different lately,"
comments Tom one day. Tom is important in the church if for no other
reason than as church treasurer he signs Pastor Bill's paycheck. "So, what's
up?" Tom asks. Pastor Bill isn't sure what to say. He feels the beginnings
of anxiety stirring within. He is never sure how to read Tom. Tom would
have been a great poker player, he thinks, except church treasurers aren't
allowed to play poker.

"Well," he stumbles, "I've been trying to put a little variety in my
preaching. You know, change things up a little."

"Why?" asks Tom the persistent.

"To make it more interesting," offers Pastor Bill. Tom doesn't look too
convinced or at least Pastor Bill thinks he doesn't look convinced. So he
quickly adds, "Like the Bible does. The Bible has stories, poems, letters,
and even the book of Revelation. I want my preaching to be more like
that, like . . . the Bible."

"Oh," says Tom. A long silence follows. Then Tom smiles (which is very
unusual for a church treasurer), "Well, I just wanted you to know that I
for one like it!"

"Thanks, Tom," says a relieved Pastor Bill. "I'm glad you like it." And to
himself he reflects, *Maybe I* am *going in the right direction.*

Sometimes I am asked what kind of Christian I am. Like many people, I am not always comfortable with titles. But still, people ask. My denomination is small and most have never heard of us, so naming my denomination is not usually helpful. Sometimes I will say, "We are like Baptists or Presbyterians" ("—the best of both," I say with a smile). But a better label I often use is *evangelical*. I like this label because it means I am a Christian who believes and lives according to the gospel. The gospel is the theological center of Scripture. So I am evangelical.

In the preceding chapters, I have explained that sermon design should be evangelical, that is, faithful to the gospel it seeks to communicate. The gospel is the final arbitrator of sermon form. Although there is no such thing as the right sermon form, there are forms that are less evangelical and forms that are more evangelical. We must hold all our efforts at sermon form up to the light of the gospel.

Not all sermon shapes are equally faithful to the gospel. Not every speech form that the human imagination can create is an appropriate vehicle for the Word of God. Some sermon designs should be used sparingly and some not at all. For instance, sermons which are too incomplete may be unfaithful to the gospel. Years ago, in an attempt at creativity I once gave a sermon that consisted primarily of a fictional story that I had written, which ended with a very brief reading from Scripture. This experiment in story preaching, I believe, failed. My form was not faithful to the text. The form failed to do justice to the idea of the text. It failed to take into account my audience, who came with certain expectations. And no amount of creativity could rescue it. The problem was with the form. The text (and the audience) demanded explanation and application. There was content that needed to be explored, but my form was not up to the challenge. Some forms with some texts in some rhetorical contexts may not be evangelical.

Sermon forms do not come tagged *evangelical* or *not-evangelical*. So we need to ask, How do we choose sermon designs that are faithful to the gospel?

Sermon Focus

An evangelical approach to sermon form will fulfill the sermon's *focus* (the central idea of the sermon and the purpose of the sermon—more on this in chapter 7). The design for any particular sermon should communicate the idea of the text and fulfill the purpose of the sermon in the life of the listeners. Haddon Robinson says, "If your development communicates your message, by all means use it; if it gets in the way of your message, then devise a form more in keeping with the idea and purpose of the Scriptures and the needs of your hearers."[1] This approach is not committed to any particular form but is committed to communicating the message in the form that best fulfills the intention of the text and of the sermon.

Fred Craddock, who began much of the modern discussion about sermon form, states that the creation of a form should flow out of the answer to the question, "What is the major communicative burden of this sermon?"[2] A sermon design that is evangelical will fulfill the sermon's focus.

Theological

An evangelical approach to sermon design will also be deeply theological. It will seek to understand the theological issues related to form (see chapter 3), and it will take the text seriously as the infallible Word of God. It is not a coincidence that homileticians who have doubts about the veracity of Scripture have tended toward forms that are more experiential and less conducive to propositional truth. It is not that those forms (story, narrative, and inductive) are always wrong. On the contrary, they are often just what is needed. But when those forms are chosen because the preacher is not confident that the Bible speaks a clear word from God, the forms may become unfaithful to the text. I believe that most forms can communicate propositional truth.

Sermon design is ultimately a theological task, and an evangelical approach to form will take seriously the issues of theology.

Further, an evangelical approach to form will seek to both *say* something and *do* something. The sermon will have both a central idea and a purpose. Our theology of preaching will not build a wall between idea and event, as if we must choose between them. An evangelical approach will seek to convey biblical truth, and it will seek to help the listener experience the gospel. Each sermon should have an idea or proposition it is seeking to convey. But an evangelical approach to form will not be satisfied with only conveying information. It will also want to do something in the life of the listener. Our sermon design will seek to be both informative and transformative. We will want the listener to understand the gospel and to experience it.

Literary Form

An evangelical approach will interact with the literary genres of Scripture (see chapter 4). I find it intriguing that evangelicals have often given much less consideration to the question of literary genre as it relates to sermon form than those who are less evangelical in their theology. One might have expected evangelicals to possess the greater concern. Robinson is one evangelical homiletician who recognizes the need for serious consideration of the literary form. He says, "Part of exegesis is to recognize that the form of literature ought to have some influence on the form of the sermon."[3]

Literary form is not determinative for the issue of sermon form, but we should always seek to allow the genre of the text to influence the form of the sermon. We should always wrestle with the question, What is the literary genre of this text and how should that genre influence the form of this sermon? The shape of the sermon should arise from the shape of the gospel.

Culturally Relevant

An evangelical approach to sermon form will be concerned with relevance to today's culture. Relevance must take a backseat to theology, but it does get a seat. Relevance is relevant! Who wants to be irrelevant? An evangelical approach will seek to understand the world in which we live and design sermons that are effective in communicating to that world. Sermons are different today than they were a generation ago and that is at least partly because we live in a different world. We must seek to faithfully communicate to that world. In the gospel, God stepped into our world. In designing sermons for today, as ambassadors of Christ we step into the listener's world.

There are dangers here. In focusing too much on relevance, we may compromise biblical truth. Culture may influence theology. It is possible to become so culturally relevant that we become irrelevant to God and his purposes.

But the issue of relevance will not go away. The wise preacher will steer a careful course. Such preachers will always seek to be faithful to the Scripture but will do so in a way that is relevant to our world.

A concern for relevance may mean that we will often preach inductively rather than deductively—for we live in an inductive world. We will want to make use of narrative and story—for we live in a storied world. But we also want to communicate the information of the Bible, and so we may at times choose a more deductive form. For preaching, cultural relevance means taking the risk of failure as we experiment with different forms.

In our church we recently completed a series of three sermons developed around the imagery of C. S. Lewis's book *The Lion, the Witch and the Wardrobe*. We timed the series to coincide with the release of Disney's film version of Lewis's book. We titled the series "Truth Behind the Wardrobe Door" and somewhat unimaginatively called the individual sermons: "The Wardrobe," "The Witch," and "The Lion." My sermon assignment was "The Lion." I approached it as a topical sermon using a subject-completed form. Each point began "Aslan (the lion in Lewis's book) pictures . . ." And then I described some characteristic of Jesus Christ that is reflected in the character of Aslan.

Was the series successful? Not entirely, since some in our audience had neither read the book nor viewed the movie (which is a significant problem in attempting to base a sermon series on a movie). But it was successful in this respect: we took the risk of attempting to relate the gospel to our world. An evangelical approach to form will do that—it will be concerned with relating the gospel to the world in which we live.

Variety in Form

An evangelical approach to sermon design will also be varied in the forms it takes. It will not be wedded to a single form. If we are to be truly evangelical, we will not allow ourselves to get in the habit of using the same sermon design week after week. Many pastors are caught in the rut of designing sermons in one predictable way week after week after week. Some are caught in the rut of classical rhetoric; others have dug a new narrative rut. But ruts are ruts. Variety in sermon design is the spice of preaching.

Scripture

Four truths argue for the use of variety in form. First, the Scriptures themselves reflect variety. Since God has seen fit to use great variety in the genre of Scripture, it just makes sense that preachers should follow his lead. We will want our preaching to reflect the variety of genres in Scripture. Scripture is a rich tapestry of God's truth woven together to form a whole. And our preaching should reflect that.

Worldview

Second, the form of a sermon tends to shape one's worldview.[4] Problem/solution sermon forms view the world in one way, while narrative sermons tend to create a different view of life. A variety of forms will avoid the problem of teaching people to see life from only one perspective. Variety in preaching form will give the listener a more balanced worldview.

Listening Styles

Third, we should vary the form of our sermons because our listeners have different styles of listening. Calvin Miller, in arguing against the overuse of narrative preaching, warns that "in every congregation there exists a strong percentage of souls whose

life orientation is less story-oriented."⁵ This is an argument for
variety in preaching. In any congregation some are more per-
ceptually oriented, while some are more narrative oriented. In
order to meet the needs of our congregations, we must vary the
form of our sermons.

Interest

Fourth, variety is just more interesting. There can be a sameness to our preaching if we are not careful. Sermon ruts can run
deep. One sermon can begin to sound like all the others. Variety
in form will help keep your preaching fresh.

A Homiletic Journey

Sunday sermons come in many sizes and shapes. There are
bombastic, declaratory sermons that bring great conviction;
rational arguments designed to convince; gripping narratives
that make us feel that we were there; erudite teaching sermons
that grant us greater understanding; and sermons filled with
imagery that inspires and lifts us up. The mystery of preaching
is that God uses sermons of all kinds. But the nagging question
remains, What will be the shape of this week's sermon?

A few years ago my son, Jonathan, and I attempted something
new. We took a five-day hike on the Appalachian Trail in Virginia.
We had traveled that way before, but always by car. We wanted
to try something new, something challenging, and something
different. I have to admit it was one of the most difficult things
I have attempted—carrying forty-pound packs up the sides of
mountains. I often wondered if I would make it. Yet it was a
worthwhile time. It gave us a completely new perspective on that
part of the country. It was very different than the view from the
interstate. It brought us together as father and son in ways that
simply driving through never could. It was so worthwhile that
we are even considering doing it again.

Stepping out into new sermonic forms may be something
new for you. It may be different and difficult. It involves some
risk. But I believe you and your listeners will also find that it is
worthwhile.

I hope that at this point you are convinced that there are theological, literary, cultural, and common sense reasons for considering different forms for sermon structure. I hope that you are ready to try something new. But that raises the question of how we can put this evangelical approach to sermon design into practice. The homiletic journey is not complete until we know *how* to create sermon designs. That is the concern of part 2.

DESIGNING
THE SERMON

Much of the apprehension that arises from attempting different sermon forms comes from not knowing how to approach the process of sermon design in creative ways. The gulf between theory and practice can be vast. It is one thing to see value in different forms; it is quite another to attempt to use them. When we find a form that works, we tend to stay with it. Better the tried-and-true, we think, than the uncertainty of the unknown. Week after week we design similar sermons, regardless of the genre of the text or the preaching situation. After a while our minds automatically form sermons in certain ways. We unconsciously impose a certain design template upon the text.

What we need is a way of approaching sermon design that will give us freedom to be flexible in our structure. The sermon design needs to flow from the text, not be imposed on it. Form should indeed follow function.

In this second section of the book, we want to discuss a basic process of sermon design that will give us maximum flexibility for sermon structure. Of course, sermon design is more art than science. There is no guaranteed method that will always produce creative sermon designs. Yet it is important to have a step-by-step approach that will allow for creativity and flexibility in the sermon process.

And process is important. Process is the route we take to arrive at our homiletic destination. Process has to do with the progress of our thought. All preachers have a process of one sort or another. But sometimes our sermonic method bypasses the design stage. We go directly from the study of the text to a particular sermon form without serious consideration of why we use that particular form. There can be such a sense of relief at identifying three or four preachable points that we fail to give the design step sufficient attention. We need a process that will enable us to think more deeply about sermon design. The right process will allow for creativity and variety in our preaching.

The Role of the Holy Spirit and Prayer

Before we consider the sermon design process in detail, something should be said about the role of the Holy Spirit and prayer in designing the sermon. The Spirit, of course, is beyond our control (see John 3:8). He shows up at unexpected times and in unexpected ways. But the preacher can at least be aware of the need for the Spirit's help in all phases of the sermon design. We should form the sermon with conscious dependence on the Holy Spirit.

One way we express that dependence is through prayer. We should begin the sermon development process with focused prayer, inviting the Spirit of God into the sermon design process. Along the way we will often pray short prayers, asking for God's help. And we will conclude, not just with a sense of relief, but with a prayer of thanksgiving for the Spirit's involvement. And in the end we will recognize that God has been at work in the sermon process.

When we are aware of the role of the Spirit and prayer we can approach the sermon design process with confidence.

Four Phases

We can identify four distinct phases in the sermon development process:

1. From text to sermon focus. This is the concern of chapter 7. The sermon focus includes the exegetical idea, the homiletical idea, and the sermon purpose. The sermon focus is the place to begin.
2. From focus to sermon form. This is often the most difficult and demanding part of the homiletic journey. This phase of the sermon process will be the major emphasis of chapters 8, 9, and 10. Chapter 8 discusses a basic approach for arriving at sermon form, chapter 9 considers some standard approaches to form, and chapter 10 looks at designing the narrative sermon.
3. Developing the sermon form. Once a basic form has been designed, that form must be expanded or developed. This is the concern of chapter 11.
4. Delivering the sermon. This part of the sermon process is not directly addressed in this book.

7

IDENTIFYING THE SERMON FOCUS

From Text to Focus	From Focus to Form	Developing the Sermon	Delivering the Sermon

I have a conviction that no sermon is ready for preaching, not ready for writing out, until we can express its theme in a short, pregnant sentence as clear as crystal. I find the getting of that sentence is the hardest, the most exacting, and the most fruitful labour in my study. To compel oneself to fashion that sentence, to dismiss every word that is vague, ragged, ambiguous, to think oneself through to a form of words which defines the theme with scrupulous exactness—this is surely one of the most vital and essential factors in the making of a sermon: and I do not think any sermon ought to be preached or even written, until that sentence has emerged, clear and lucid as a cloudless moon.

J. H. Jowett, *The Preacher: His Life and Work*

I have a friend who, with his family, sets out on vacation without a clear destination in mind. They just drive and where they end up is where they end up. It makes for some interesting vacations. While that may be okay for a vacation trip, it is not a good procedure for sermon design. Yet some preachers approach sermon design like my friend takes vacations: they set out to design a sermon without any clear idea of where the sermon is going.

The Sermon Focus

The place to begin in sermon design is with the sermon focus. As every journey needs a map, so every sermon needs a focus. The sermon focus consists of the exegetical idea of the sermon, the homiletical idea, and the sermon's purpose. The exegetical idea is the central thought or proposition of the text. The exegetical idea is "what the biblical author was saying to his readers."[1] The homiletical idea is the exegetical idea written for today's audience. It is sometimes called the "big idea."[2] The purpose is what the sermon intends to do in the life of the listener. It is the goal of the sermon. Together these form what I call the *focus* of the sermon.

In recent homiletical thought there has been much debate over whether a sermon should communicate an idea or facilitate an event. What do we bring across the homiletical bridge (if there even is a homiletical bridge)? Is the homiletic payoff an idea in propositional form or is it an experience of the gospel? Some modern homileticians have rejected the idea of a propositional idea or theme for a sermon. They point out that a sermon ought to be directed toward the heart and the will. But consider Jesus's statement "Love the Lord your God with all your heart and with all your soul and with all your mind" (Matt. 22:37). That is a proposition. It is an idea. It has a subject, a verb, and an object. But it is not just an idea. It is an idea that should affect both the heart and the mind. It is an idea that ought to transform life. You simply cannot communicate without propositions.

On the other side of the issue are homileticians or preachers who sound as if preaching is just the communication of information about the Bible. For them, preaching is propositional; it is explanation with some application.

Some homileticians focus on the sermon as an event while others emphasize the propositional nature of preaching. Why not both? The sermon must both say something and do something. There is no inherent conflict between the sermon as idea and the sermon as event. Something can be learned from both camps. Thus, the sermon will have focus: an idea and a purpose.

It is important that we identify the sermon focus before we attempt to develop the sermon design. The sermon must have a clearly defined idea and destination before a structure can be created. One of the pitfalls to avoid in sermon design is attempting to sketch out the form of the sermon before we have determined the direction the sermon must go. It is like taking a trip without a destination in mind or shooting a gun without aiming it. The temptation to move toward the particulars of sermon design prematurely must be resisted.

Often in my study, early on, I will think of a way that the sermon might be designed. I don't ignore that thought—it could turn out to be gold. I write it down and set it aside for consideration after I have determined the sermon focus. Once the sermon focus has been formulated, I return to those thoughts about design. Sometimes my early thoughts turn out to be just right, and I use them—sometimes in modified form. At other times it becomes clear that the initial attempt at design will not communicate a sermon's idea or fulfill its purpose. But I cannot make that determination until I have a clearly defined focus for the sermon.

The focus is key to the organization of the sermon. The focus is the structural center for the sermon. We have to know where we are going in the homiletic journey before we can determine how to get there. Together the homiletical idea and the purpose will give direction to our design.

For a recent emergency trip to visit my wife's family (due to my father-in-law's death), we had to make a decision about how to travel: to fly or drive. There were pros and cons to each mode of transportation. We were greatly helped in the decision-making process by knowing how much time we had for the trip and a clear destination: the state of Florida (a two-day drive from our home). Given the time and destination, it quickly became clear that the only way to travel was by plane. In the same way, a clear sermon focus can help to determine the design of the sermon. The sermon focus gives the preacher a direction and a destination. So the first major movement in sermon development is to arrive at a clear sermon focus. When we study we should always have a goal—to identify the homiletical idea and the purpose of the sermon.

Begin with a Text or Topic

Expository preaching must be firmly anchored in the text. Three approaches to the text of Scripture are typically employed. We may begin with a particular preaching passage, or we may begin with a topic and move to a single passage, or we may begin with a topic and go to multiple passages. These three approaches can yield two types of expository sermons: the single text expository sermon and the topical expository sermon (an expository sermon based on multiple texts).

In the pages ahead I will focus on sermons based on a single preaching passage of Scripture. This is for two reasons: first, explaining everything from two different perspectives is cumbersome, and second, preaching from a single passage ought to be our primary (though not exclusive) approach to preaching. A possible way to divide up the preaching task is to preach half of the time using sermons in a continuous series through books of the Bible, a quarter of the time using topical series but preaching from single passages of Scripture, and a quarter of the time using topical expository sermons. Although most of what follows will assume a single preaching passage, much of it can and should apply to topical exposition as well.

Part of determining the text is to identify the limits of the preaching passage. This will involve a study of the passage and its context. We will attempt to clearly identify where the preaching passage begins and where it ends. The preaching portion may be as short as a few verses or in some cases as long as several chapters. Since the sermon focus should arise out of a study of the sermon's text, the first stop on the journey toward form is to identify the text for the sermon. This will be done through our own study of the text and the appropriate use of commentaries.

Discover the Exegetical Idea

When we study a passage we are not wandering aimlessly through a homiletic wasteland. We have a destination in mind—an idea. Expository preaching is the communication of a central thought. That is not all it is, but it is at least that. Even when a sermon is narrative or inductive in form, it should still embody a significant idea. The sermon is propositional at its core.[3] Once we have identified a text, our study should be focused on determining the central idea.

The central idea is very important in preaching. Nearly all homileticians agree that a sermon must have one central unifying thought. It is the central idea that gives the sermon focus. A sermon with three separate ideas is really three sermons. For the biblical expositor, that central idea must come from Scripture.

In *Design for Preaching*, H. Grady Davis explains that "a well-prepared sermon is the embodiment, the development, the full statement of a significant thought."[4] Thomas Long contends that the central idea is "what the whole sermon will be about."[5] At the end of the study process we should be able to write out the central idea of the sermon in a single clear sentence.

Regardless of where we begin (whether with a topic or a text), ultimately in expository preaching the direction of movement will be from the text to the central idea. The Scripture is not used to simply reinforce the idea or ideas of the preacher but is rather the source of the idea or ideas for the sermon. This is critical if we are to avoid the common temptation of proof-texting—using the Scripture to support what we want to say or what we think our audience wants us to say. Regardless of how the material may ultimately be packaged, the central idea must spring from the passage or passages being studied.

The central idea can be expressed in two ways. The first is called the exegetical idea, and the second is called the homiletical idea. The exegetical idea is the product of the exegetical study of the text. The exegetical idea seeks to answer the question, What is this passage saying? The exegetical idea can be cast in the past tense. "This is what the apostle Paul said about this topic . . ." Or, "Here is what Joshua chapter 1 communicated to the Israelites." At this point we are not yet concerned with the contemporary audience. The exegetical idea is concerned with the intent of the author in relation to the biblical audience. The exegetical idea is the central idea in biblical dress. The two parts of the exegetical idea are the subject and the complement.

The Subject

The subject is the complete, definite answer to the question, What am I talking about? The subject should never be a single word because a single-word subject is too broad. The subject is best expressed in a phrase.

Incorrect Examples of the Subject	Correct Examples of the Subject
Prayer	How to pray effectively
Salvation	Why you need to be saved
Holiness	The benefits of holiness

The examples on the left above do not form homiletic subjects because they are not the full, definite answers to the question, What am I talking about? They are too general. You can't preach as focused a sermon on "prayer" as you can a sermon on "how to pray effectively."

The Complement

The complement is the answer to the question, What is this writer saying about what he's talking about?[6] The complement completes the subject. It answers the question asked in the subject. "How can we pray effectively?" may be our subject. The complement could be: "when we persist in prayer." Put together, the exegetical idea would be: "We pray effectively when we persist in prayer."

The complement can be a single statement or it may consist of multiple statements. In general, a single complement sermon has greater unity and clarity. But at times when there are multiple assertions about a particular subject, the complement will consist of multiple statements. This is especially true when the biblical text contains some kind of list. One popular example of a multiple complement sermon form is the subject-completed sermon. In this oft-used form the subject is introduced at the beginning of the sermon and then the main points complete the subject.

Example of a Subject and a Complement
Psalm 117

Praise the LORD, all you nations;
    extol him, all you peoples.
For great is his love toward us,
    and the faithfulness of the LORD endures forever.

Praise the LORD.

Subject: why we should praise the Lord
Complement: because of his faithful love

A Significant Idea

It is important to remember that we are looking for a significant idea. Not every idea presented in the Scripture is of equal weight. Haddon Robinson believes that there are only eight or nine "great" ideas in the Bible restated in many ways.[7] We may not always have a "great" idea for our sermon, but we need to be sure that it is a significant one. If the idea is not significant, it will not be able to bear the weight of the sermon. A significant idea will capture the heart and the mind. It will preach! A significant idea will give burning focus to the sermon. If we do not have a significant idea, we have several options: continue the study of the passage until we identify such an idea, consider preaching on a different text, or call in a guest preacher.

Together the subject and complement should form the full exegetical idea of the text. The exegetical idea is the culmination of the first phase of sermon development. It is the fruit of our study. And it is the necessary foundation for sermon design.

Develop the Homiletical Idea

Once we have identified the exegetical idea we can then develop the homiletical idea, which is the exegetical idea expressed in contemporary dress. The exegetical idea is the main idea of the text, whereas the homiletical idea is the main idea of the sermon. The homiletical idea brings the exegetical idea into the twenty-first century and reshapes the exegetical idea for today's audience.

The homiletical idea must cross the bridge between biblical times and contemporary life. It must make the hermeneutical trip from text to audience. The homiletical idea is, to borrow philosopher Hans-Georg Gadamer's phrase, the "fusion of two horizons": the horizon of the text and the horizon of the contemporary listener. It should be written as clearly and carefully as possible, and it should be written as a single sentence. Once the homiletical idea is formulated, we have the entire sermon summed up in a single, concise, clearly written statement.

There are two issues to keep firmly in mind in developing the homiletical idea. First, the homiletical idea must grow out of the exegetical idea. The exegetical idea is the foundation upon which the homiletical idea must be built. The relationship between the two should be clear. Second, the homiletical idea must take into account the contemporary listener. Here is where the audience becomes part of the sermon process. There is a sense in which the listener is always a part of the sermon process, because preachers go to the text as representatives of the church. But at this point in the process we involve the listener in a more explicit way. We ask, What is this text saying to this audience? Answering this question helps us write the homiletical idea with today's audience in mind.

At times the homiletical idea and the exegetical idea will be substantially the same. When the exegetical idea expresses a universal principle, which is not bound by time or culture, the homiletical idea may be very similar to the exegetical idea. But even in those instances it is best to write the homiletical idea in a way that is as audience-specific as possible. For a sermon on Ephesians 1, I wrote the following exegetical idea: "We should praise God because he has given us every spiritual blessing in Christ." My homiletical idea was not far different: "We should bless God because he has blessed us." Because the passage presents universal truths, the exegetical idea and the homiletical idea were very similar.

The Homiletical Idea Should Be Personal

There are three guidelines in developing the homiletical idea. First, a good homiletical idea is personal. The homiletical idea differs from the exegetical idea in terms of the audience with whom it is concerned. The exegetical idea is concerned with the message to the recipients of that day; the homiletical idea has a specific contemporary audience in mind and addresses contemporary concerns. It is usually written in the second person or the first person plural. It is also written to the church at First and Main. The closer we come to the individual in the pew the better. The homiletical idea tells us what the text is saying to today's audience—and to this particular audience.

The Homiletical Idea Should Be Contemporary

Second, a good homiletical idea is contemporary. It uses the language of today. The homiletical idea should be either timeless or contemporary in its orientation. The homiletical idea differs from the exegetical idea in its time perspective. The exegetical idea is usually written in the past tense; the homiletical idea is written in the present tense and uses contemporary language. The homiletical idea cries, "Here is what this text is saying today!" Though we begin in biblical times, we cannot stay there. Preaching is a present tense event.

The Homiletical Idea Should Be Memorable

Third, a good homiletical idea is memorable. It should be expressed clearly and use imaginative language. This idea should sparkle. With the exegetical idea, we strive for precision. With the homiletical idea, we work for creativity in expression. A well-written homiletical idea gives us something worth saying—indeed, something we have to say. The homiletical idea should capture the imagination.

The essential difference, then, between the exegetical idea and the homiletical idea is the audience in view. The exegetical idea is concerned with the audience of two thousand (or more) years ago and how they would apply the text; the homiletical idea is concerned with the audience today and how we should apply the text.

The following is an example of a homiletical idea from 1 Peter 2:18–19:

> *Exegetical Idea:* Slaves should submit to their masters even when they are harsh, because of their awareness of God's presence and will.
>
> *Homiletical Idea:* You should submit to those who have authority over you even when they are difficult, because you know that God is there and he has a purpose for you.

In the example above, the homiletical idea and the exegetical idea are different, yet there is a clear connection between them. Note that while the exegetical idea is written in the third person, the homiletical idea is written in the second person; writing this idea in the first person plural is another possibility. Also, notice that while the exegetical idea was written from the perspective of the biblical text (slaves and masters), the homiletical idea was written using the present tense and related to present-day audiences.

Since the homiletical idea is the exegetical idea re-formed, once the homiletical idea is clearly formulated, the exegetical idea can be left behind. The exegetical idea is really the first phase in discovering the homiletical idea. Like the rockets that are jettisoned once the space shuttle is in orbit, so the exegetical idea can be abandoned once the homiletical idea is formulated. It is the homiletical idea that will be important for sermon design.

Identify the Purpose

We have carefully formulated the homiletical idea. But there is still another stop to make before we arrive at the completed sermon focus and are ready to move to sermon design. We must determine the sermon's purpose. The purpose is the final destination of the sermon. Bill Hybels suggests that preachers should always ask what they want the listener to know and what they want the listener to do.[8] Purpose has to do with what we want the listener to do. The purpose statement tells us where we are going. I have occasionally come to the end of the sermon process and realized to my chagrin that I didn't know how I wanted my listeners to respond! In my eagerness to write the sermon I had failed to write out the sermon's purpose. In the purpose statement, we answer the question, What do I want my listeners to do because of this sermon?

In determining the purpose for the sermon, we must first discover the purpose of the text. Ask questions such as: Why is this text in the Bible? What is it doing? What is its function? What was the author's purpose for his readers in writing this text? The purpose of the sermon will flow from the purpose of the text. Before we can determine the sermon's purpose, we must have a clear understanding of the text's purpose.

Once we have identified the text's purpose we develop the purpose for the sermon. This purpose statement must be stated in light of the particular audience that you will be addressing. The circumstances of your audience are not identical to those of the biblical audience. There will probably be similarities but there will often be significant differences. So you will have your contemporary audience in mind as you formulate your purpose statement. Though your purpose statement will probably not be identical to the purpose of the biblical writer, it should correspond closely with it. They both should be going in the same general direction.

The purpose will most often be written in terms of specific, observable behavior. Some sermons may have as their purpose that the listener would think differently about a certain subject or believe differently. But most of the time the purpose can still identify what the listener will do differently because they think or believe differently. So we ask, How would the listener's life be impacted by this sermon? What will the person sitting in the pew actually do because of this sermon? How will the one listening put it into practice? If the preacher doesn't know what the listener should do in response to the sermon, the chances are good that the listener won't either! A good purpose statement uses active verbs and is written in terms of performance, what the listeners will do, or the results of what they will do. Good purposes are also stated in narrow terms, that is, with words that are not subject to many different understandings.[9] The goal is specificity. Together with the homiletical idea, the purpose forms the sermon focus.

Here is an example of a purpose statement for Psalm 117.

Subject: why we should praise the Lord

Complement: because of his faithful love

Purpose: that the listener would recognize and express the great value of the Lord because of his faithful love

The Next Step

We have arrived at the point in the sermon preparation process where we have a clear sermon focus: a homiletical idea and a purpose. The sermon focus concludes the exegetical phase of sermon development. Now what do we do with the focus? We organize the sermon around it. Everything that is said and done in the sermon should lead up to the statement of the idea of the sermon or flow from it. And everything in the sermon should work to fulfill the purpose. This is the biblical foundation upon which the sermon design must be built. Because these two are so foundational for designing the sermon, it is a helpful habit to type the homiletical idea and the purpose for the sermon at the top of your manuscript or outline. These two are the keys that will open the door to sermon form. Whatever design you ultimately choose should communicate the idea of the sermon and fulfill the sermon's purpose.

DESIGNING THE
BASIC FORM

From Text to Focus	From Focus to Form	Developing the Sermon	Delivering the Sermon

A man determined to preach his best has before him, like any artist, a lifelong struggle with form.

H. Grady Davis, *Design for Preaching*

One of the most perplexing questions of the sermon craft is how to form the sermon. How one takes a text and the scribbling of exegetical labor and forms it into a sermon for Sunday morning is perhaps the most creative and frustrating aspect of the sermon task. Bryan Chapell says that as he talks with pastors, questions about structure are the questions most often asked.[1] And with good reason—each sermon needs a structure. Without a good structure, the sermon process cannot proceed. So, which structure? There may be questions of greater theological weight, but few are as practically pressing.

At this point we have a text and a central idea and even a sermon purpose. It is not yet a sermon. What do we do with our thoughts? How do we form our thoughts into a cohesive whole? How do we develop this idea from this text into a sermon? The purpose of this chapter is to help us think through the basic process of sermon form development. Chapters 9 and 10 will further elucidate the basic approach (chapter 9 focusing on the various forms available and chapter 10 on how we form narrative sermons). Together these chapters present the second phase of our sermon process: moving from focus to form.

Sermon Form Basics

All sermons have structure. There is no such thing as a formless sermon. It is impossible to preach without form. Even chaos is a kind of form. As the body needs a skeleton, so the sermon needs a structure. And the form you choose makes a difference. One can hardly make progress in sermon development until the basic question of form is answered.

Sermon Form Is an Organizational Plan

Sermon form involves several components: the content to be communicated, the manner in which it will be spoken, and the sequence in which it will be delivered. The sermon is like a trip, complete with a destination, stops along the way, and decisions to be made about sequence of travel. Thomas Long says, "A sermon form is an organizational plan for deciding what kinds of things will be said and done in a sermon and in what sequence."[2] This plan is called the outline or (more recently by some homileticians) the plot of the sermon. The sermon form tells us what has to happen in this sermon to communicate the idea and to accomplish the purpose.

Sermon Form Is the Reshaping of Scripture

In reality all preaching involves a reshaping. Scripture comes to us in various literary forms, each with a particular literary purpose. The sermon must reshape Scripture into sermonic (oral) form. This is not because Scripture is in any sense insufficient, but because a sermon is a different (spoken) medium of communication. Texts do not come to us complete with sermon structures attached. Rarely, if ever, is a text structured with three or four points in parallel form. But the text does have a structure. It will often have a narrative structure, sometimes a poetic form, or at times it will have a didactic design. The sermon reshapes the written form of the text into the oral form of the sermon. Thus, the form of the sermon will not necessarily be the same as the form of the text. The preacher will redesign a given text to fulfill the purpose of the sermon and communicate its idea. In the end all sermon form is a creative act of the preacher.[3]

Sermon Form Is Critical to Listener Response

The form of the sermon is key to the response of the listener. Sidney Greidanus reminds us that "some forms are more likely than others to elicit praise, or surprise, or assent, or change, or enthusiasm."[4] Consider the following well-known beginnings: "Dearly beloved, we are gathered here today . . ."; "Once upon a time . . ."; "There were these two Irishmen . . ." Each of these stock forms serves to shape the response and the expectation of the listener. They prepare us to respond in a certain way: for a wedding ceremony, a story, and a joke.

A sermon that begins as a story may cue its listeners to sit back and listen to the story unfold. A sermon that starts with

"I want to share with you four reasons why . . ." may cause the listener to take out a pen and prepare to take notes. Some forms will hold interest better than others. An inductive form, which holds the main point of the sermon until the end, may more easily keep interest than a deductive design. Some forms require more listener involvement. An open-ended sermon will require more participation than a sermon form that clearly spells everything out. When we ask questions about form, we are asking how we want our listeners to respond.

Sermon Form Influences Worldview

The form of the sermon can begin to shape the listener's view of life. Or perhaps a better way to put it is that form can affect the listener's faith perspective. Listening to problem/solution sermons on a regular basis can cause people to view the Christian life as a problem in need of a solution. A consistent either/or pattern can lead to a black-and-white view of life.

A steady diet of sermons which give us "five reasons" or "four keys" or "six benefits" may create a rationalistic view of life. "Form is so extremely important," affirms Fred Craddock. "Regardless of the subjects being treated, a preacher can thereby nourish rigidity or openness, legalism or graciousness, inclusiveness or exclusiveness, adversarial or conciliating mentality, willingness to discuss or demand immediate answers."[5]

Designing the Basic Form

My son works for L'Oreal, the cosmetic company. He is a process engineer. A process engineer, as best I understand it, designs the processes by which certain ingredients are combined in specific quantities at specific temperatures to form a particular product. Preachers need to be homiletic process engineers. They combine the basic ingredients of a sermon (exegesis, theology, audience analysis, and life experience) and form them into a particular homiletic pattern. Preachers need a procedure to follow.

There is, of course, no seven-step, sure-fire method that will invariably lead to just the right sermon structure. Sermon design is messier than that. Designing sermons is a creative act of the preacher under the direction of the Holy Spirit. Somehow it happens each Sunday, and often we don't know how.

And yet something can and must be said about how to approach this creative endeavor. There are basic steps and thought processes that can guide us in thinking through the process that is necessary for creative sermon design. All good preachers have a way of thinking about sermon design, oftentimes intuitively. In this section we want to expose to the light of homiletic day the kind of thinking that needs to go into sermon design. We are concerned here with the "thinking through" process that moves us toward form. We need to have an approach that respects the text, allows for flexibility and creativity in the design of the sermon, and collaborates with the work of the Holy Spirit.

The previous chapter gave us the result of the first phase of the sermon: the sermon focus. Here we now suggest five steps that can guide us through the next phase: the sermon design.

Step 1: Begin with the Sermon Focus

Where do we start? Begin with the fruit of your exegetical labors: the homiletical idea and the purpose of the sermon. Together these two form the focus of the sermon. The focus is the organizing key for sermon design. It gives us the direction and the destination of the sermon. In the homiletic journey the homiletical idea is the compass, and the purpose is our destination. Together they can help us chart a course.

Think deeply about the homiletical idea and the purpose. Ask how this idea can be best communicated and this purpose best accomplished.[6] What needs to be said to get this idea across and to fulfill the intention of the sermon? The homiletical idea and the purpose are the controlling factors in the development of the sermon form. Everything that is said in the sermon should relate to the idea and purpose of the sermon. The main points of the sermon will either lead to the central idea or flow from it. Everything should work to fulfill the purpose. The sermon focus is what gives the sermon unity.

Haddon Robinson contends that there are four and only four things which can be done to develop any idea: it can be restated, explained, proved, or applied.[7] Three of these four concepts give us developmental questions[8] that can help us probe the sermon idea and move us forward in the sermon design process.

RESTATEMENT

Restatement means to state the same thing using different words. Restatement functions to reinforce an idea. Restatement does not give us new information. Restatement is very important in the final stages of preparation and in the delivery of the sermon but is not particularly helpful at this early stage of sermon development.

EXPLANATION

Explanation asks, What does this mean? This is the first developmental question. In every text there is something to be explained, so this question is always relevant. But some texts beg for explanation as the primary focus. So we ask, What needs to be explained in this text? What will my audience not understand? Is the author of the text developing his thought primarily through explanation? This developmental question may lead toward a sermon that is primarily explanatory.

PROOF

The third way to develop an idea is to prove it. This gives us the second developmental question, Is it true? This question wrestles with the validity of the idea. In some texts the author is attempting to prove his point. And some audiences need to have the truth of the text proven to them. In such instances, a sermon may focus on proving the central idea. In applying this question to the sermon, we ask, Is this passage seeking to prove an idea? Is this an idea that must be demonstrated to be true to my audience?

APPLICATION

Lastly, we can apply an idea. This leads to the third developmental question, What difference does it make? It asks, "So what?" This developmental question can lead to a sermon that applies. Application is relating the truth of the passage to the lives of the hearers. Application is showing the listener how this idea can be put into practice. Sometimes the application to contemporary audiences is the same as to the first-century audience. But often the cultural situation of the text is significantly different from the contemporary culture. The preacher must show how this text, which applied to the original hearers in a certain way, can now be legitimately applied to the life and situation of today's hearers. Every sermon will have application, but some sermons may have application as the primary focus.

These developmental questions can help us think about the homiletical idea of the sermon. The sermon focus is the place to begin. So spend some time with the homiletical idea and the sermon purpose.

Step 2: Do a Structural Analysis of the Text

It is helpful at this point in the sermon preparation process to do a structural analysis of the passage. We want the text to have a controlling influence on our sermon form. A structural analysis can help that happen. To analyze the structure of the text we consider the ideas of the text, follow the twists and turns of logic in the text, and plot the sequence of thought. The structural analysis will show the flow of thought in the preaching passage. To identify the divisions of the text and the logic that connects them, write out a one-sentence description for each division in the preaching passage. The original author had a rhetorical design. The preacher's task is to identify that design.

Oftentimes the movement of thought in the text will help to determine the movement of thought in the sermon. The sermon does not have to duplicate the flow of thought in the text, but it often will. Fred Craddock maintains that even when the form of the sermon does not follow the form of the text, it should still be "congenial to the message and experience of the text."[9] Consider the following structural analysis I completed for a sermon from a text in Romans.

A Structural Analysis of Romans 3:9–24

Verse 9: Paul makes a generalization based on Romans 1:18–3:8 that all are under sin.

Verses 10–18: Paul proves the generalization by quoting a number of Old Testament Scriptures which point out the sinfulness of humanity.

Verses 19–20: Paul explains that the law, rather than justifying us, functions to make us conscious of sin.

Verses 21–24: But we can be justified because a righteousness from God is now revealed.

A sermon design for Romans 3:9–24 may very well follow the general course of the text.

In this step we will also be concerned with the genre of the text. Is it apocalyptic, epistle, or psalm? How should the genre of the text influence the form of the sermon?[10] More will be said about narrative genre in chapter 10.

Step 3: Do an Audience Analysis

Invite your audience into the sermon design process. What questions would your listeners raise about this text and this idea? Think of specific individuals with specific needs and concerns. Choose five or six people who are different in age, sex, race, and social status. Imagine them seated around your desk. Ask them how this text applies to them. What questions does it raise? What don't they understand? What do they have a hard time accepting?

Some pastors meet weekly with a group of people to discuss such questions prior to preaching a sermon—I expect to great benefit. And though most of us might find that logistically challenging, we can at least invite our audience into the process through creative imagination. Invite your listeners into your design process.

Step 4: Complete a Sermon Task List

I'm big on lists. I almost always have a list of things to do. I first make a list and then prioritize it. I don't always do everything on my list, but I try to do what is most important. The sermon design process ought to include something similar: a sermon task list.[11] The sermon task list is a list of what must be said and done in order to communicate the idea and to accomplish the purpose of the sermon. Your task list will draw from your exegetical study, your analysis of the sermon focus, the structural analysis of the text, theological reflection, and your analysis of the audience.

Brainstorming

A sermon task list may be created in two parts. The first is brainstorming. This is a time to let your imagination roam. Jot down ideas and thoughts as they occur to you. Think deeply about what needs to be said and done to fulfill the focus of this sermon. Go back over your study notes, looking for important ideas. Write down everything that you can think of. At this point, there is no such thing as a bad idea.

Theological Concern

The second part of a sermon task list involves raising theological concerns. With Chapell we too wonder how our sermon can be Christ-centered.[12] We may consider how the traditional categories of law and gospel (or trouble and grace[13]) might affect our task list. Do the theological categories of trouble and grace appear in our list? If not, why not? We will want our sermon to be Christ-centered and to present God's solution of grace to our predicament. We will ask, What needs to be said and done to accomplish these goals?

Will all of the main points come directly from the text? Much of the time they will, but there may be times when you need to explore an issue or concern or objection that relates to the text but is raised primarily by a theological concern or a concern of the audience. In a recent sermon on 1 Corinthians 9:24–27, which speaks of the race we run in life as believers, one of my points was that it is God who enables us to run the race. That thought is implied in the text, but it arose first out of a theological concern to identify the grace of God in the race we run.

In another example, a sermon task list for Romans 3:9–24 might look like this:

- show that God calls us sinners
- express the popular idea that people are good or at least good enough
- show how we see sinfulness in life
- examine the Scriptures that demonstrate our sinfulness
- explain the consequences of being sinners—we cannot be justified by the law
- explain how we can be justified

Step 5: Select and Sequence the Thought

Once we have completed the sermon task list, we have to make some decisions. This is where we attempt to identify a series of preachable ideas and order them in a particular sequence. Questions related to the sermon's direction of movement and the relationship of the text's genre to the sermon form are asked and answered at this point. We may want to consider stock forms such as problem/solution or subject-completed to see if any "just fits." We will need to wrestle with whether the sermon's movement should be primarily deductive or inductive. Theological concerns such as how this sermon can be Christ-centered must be raised. We will probably make several attempts before finding a form that works for this sermon.

It is important to remember that we do not have to discover the best possible sermon form—just one that will say and do what this sermon needs to say and do. Perfectionism can be paralyzing and the search for just the right form can at times be counterproductive. A variety of forms are possible for a given sermon.

So to summarize, step 5 involves two parts. First, you need to select the main thoughts that will form the skeleton for your sermon. Some of the ideas jotted down just need to be put aside. They may be valid ideas for another sermon on another day, but they will not fulfill this sermon's idea and purpose. Other thoughts are subordinate thoughts and will be placed under one of the main points. And a few of the ideas will be the main points upon which your sermon structure will be developed. Having the sermon focus clearly before you will help in selecting which thoughts make the cut.

Second, you must sequence your thought. Sequence relates to the order of your ideas. If you are planning a trip to several stores, you must determine the order in which you will go. Sometimes the order might seem obvious: "First, the post office, then I have to stop by the dry cleaners. Oh, and we need bread from the grocery store and ice cream for the party. I better go to the grocery store last so the ice cream won't melt." At other times the order might not be so clear. But there must be an order. So it is with preaching. In preaching you must determine the sequence you will use to accomplish the focus of the sermon. This approach to sermon form does not commit to any particular sermon pattern. It may be that the sequence of your sermon will fit nicely into a traditional deductive sermon structure with parallel ideas and wording. But perhaps the message of the text will not easily fit into that mold and will require a narrative or inductive approach. Form should follow function. You should first find out what you need to say, and then figure out how to say it.

There is more than one way in which you can sequence your thought. The order should be determined by the text, theological considerations, and the need and capacities of the listener.[14] How do I make this sermon Christ-centered? In what order does the listener need to hear this? What order makes the most sense? What is the direction of the movement for this sermon: deductive or inductive? Your sequence may reflect the sequence of the text and yet it does not need to be identical. Rhetorical considerations may cause you to choose a different sequence than the biblical writer. Even sermons using parallel points need an order (e.g., simplest first, best last, and weakest in the middle). The goal is to have a series of preachable ideas in some sort of logical order.

Sequencing the sermon's progression of thought is one of the creative aspects of the sermon and should not be hurried. Allow sufficient time for completing this thinking-through process. Typically, once I have settled on a sermon design, I experience a sense of relief. So my temptation is to rush this part of the process. But I am learning to take my time at this critical juncture. Even so, thinking things through cannot continue indefinitely. For some preachers, however, the problem is not rushing to bring closure to the process of selecting a sermon form but a paralysis that keeps them from deciding on a form to use. At some point a commitment must be made to a particular form. That initial form may end up being rearranged or refined as the sermon's preparation progresses, but having a form with which to work is a place to begin.

Applying the Basic Steps

We have suggested a five-step process for sermon design: (1) begin with the sermon focus, (2) do a structural analysis of the text, (3) do an audience analysis, (4) complete a sermon task list, and (5) select and sequence your thought. I would suggest that you make use of this process in your normal sermon preparation work. I typically use five sheets of paper, one for each of the five steps. Create a template in a word processing program, listing the steps, one at the top of each sheet of paper. Or simply write out the five steps by hand, one across the top of each sheet of paper. You can then use these five sheets to keep you on track in the sermon design process. Although these steps will not remove the hard work of sermon design, they will help you think through the issues related to design.

9

Considering
Standard Forms

| From Text to Focus | From Focus to Form | Developing the Sermon | Delivering the Sermon |

When we think through . . . all the issues about sermon form, the end result of our thinking will often be not some utterly new and wildly innovative form, but, rather, a form that has been employed by many preachers before, and quite effectively.

Thomas G. Long, *The Witness of Preaching*

Not every sermon must be created from scratch. As mentioned before, the good news is that the number of approaches to sermon design is limited. There are unlimited variations, but only so many basic approaches. Every sermon will be distinctive but not unique! Recognizing this will help preachers as they seek to design their sermons.

Let's imagine a preacher sitting at his desk. He has arrived at the sermon focus. He has completed a structural analysis. He has before him a completed sermon task list. But now he must select and sequence his thought. This can seem like an impossible task. But he does not have to walk this part of the homiletic journey alone. He walks in company with a multitude of preachers and homileticians who have gone before. He recognizes that there are only so many basic sermon forms that preachers use. In forming his sermon he will consider the various designs that are available. In this chapter we will focus on the fifth step in the basic approach to sermon form ("select and sequence your thought")—shaping a series of preaching ideas into a particular form.

The Question of Movement

One of the key issues to consider in the sermon design process is the question of movement. Sermons are not static—they are going somewhere. They have a beginning and a destination. Sermons take the listener on a journey. This question of movement comes into sharp focus when we talk of sequencing our thought. What direction will this sermon take? Every form needs to make progress in one direction or another. The two basic directions of movement in thought are deductive movement and inductive movement. Deductive movement is movement *from*. Inductive movement is movement *toward*. Like a highway in which there are only two directions to travel, every sermon must employ either deductive or inductive movement or some combination of the two. So a basic question for the preacher to wrestle with is What is the direction of movement in this sermon?

Related to movement is the issue of tension. Tension is the unresolvedness of the sermon. Tension is what keeps the listeners on the edge of their seats; it keeps them listening. This tension is what Eugene Lowry calls ambiguity.[1] Questions are asked but not answered. Problems are explored but not solved. Issues are raised but not resolved. Some sermons state the central idea early in the sermon and then ask questions about that idea, questions that simply must be answered. Other sermons develop tension by not revealing the full central idea until the end of the sermon. However it is done, a sermon must have tension! When the tension is gone, the sermon is over.

Deductive Sermon Structure

Preachers use deductive and inductive movement to create four basic structures. The first is a pure deductive structure. The movement is from the general (the central idea) to the particular (the explanation, proof, or application) of the idea. The sermon begins with the central idea and then raises questions about that idea. In a deductive sermon, the preacher states the central idea in the introduction or in the first major point of the sermon. At first glance, this might seem to remove any tension from the sermon. But tension can be maintained by asking significant questions. Haddon Robinson suggests that there are three basic kinds of deductive approaches: sermons that seek to explain, sermons that seek to prove, and sermons that seek to apply.[2] The key to forming the deductive sermon type is asking the right questions—questions which the listener might raise.

A great illustration of deductive movement is the old *Columbo* television mysteries. You always knew early on "who did it." The big question was how Columbo, the detective, would prove it. This is movement from the general thought (who did it) to the particulars (how Columbo would prove it). Such movement is opposite of the movement in most murder mysteries in which the conclusion (who did it) is not revealed until the very end of the story (inductive movement).

In a sermon that I heard recently, the preacher gave his main thought in his introduction—"being a Christian means being committed." The remainder of the sermon, through illustration, exhortation, and explanation, attempted to explain, prove, and apply that simple thought. To do so, he employed deductive movement.

Since deductive sermons tend to be an analysis of the central idea, the main points of the sermon link back to the central idea rather than to the preceding points. The main points will most often be written in parallel form with parallel logic. The flow of thought is from the central idea to the particular in each case. Since each point flows from the central idea (given in the introduction) rather than the preceding point, the order of ideas is less significant than it is in inductive movement. Often the sequence of the main points is interchangeable. Deductive preaching "announces general, propositional conclusions and then breaks them down into various points and exhortations."[3]

The most obvious advantage to deductive movement is clarity. The deductive form begins with a full statement of the central idea. It then clarifies that statement by explaining, proving, and/or applying it. It often ends with some form of restatement of the central idea. In a deductive sermon, we "tell them what we are going to tell them, then we tell them, then we tell them what we told them." The deductive form is nothing if not clear.

Done badly the deductive form can lead to a loss of interest by the listener. The way to avoid that loss of interest is to ask significant questions, questions the listener will want answered.

When do we make use of the deductive sermon form? Don Sunukjian suggests that the time to use deductive structure is when the statement of the main idea "automatically raises questions in the listener's mind."[4] The structure of the sermon then seeks to answer those questions. We take our cue from the listener.

What could a deductive sermon look like? The structure might look like this:

Example of a Deductive Sermon Structure

Introduction
Central Sermon Idea
I. First Main Point
   A. Development 1
   B. Development 2

II. Second Main Point
   A. Development 1
   B. Development 2
Conclusion
Restatement of the Central Idea

Here is an example of a deductive sermon structure for a specific text.

"How to Get Along with Your Parents"

Sermon on Ephesians 6:1–3

Homiletical idea: Your responsibility in the family is to obey your parents.

1. Your responsibility is to obey your parents (*full statement of homiletical idea*).

Transition: Why should you obey them?

2. You should obey your parents because that is part of what it means to be a Christian.

3. You should obey your parents because it is the right thing to do.

4. You should obey your parents because it honors your parents.

5. You should obey your parents because it is good for you.

In this sermon, which was directed toward the children of the church, I gave the full idea in the first point: you should obey your parents. In the transition between points 1 and 2 I said, "Of course, you have heard that before. But maybe what you haven't heard is why you should obey them." And then I gave four reasons why children should obey. I was raising the question, Is it really true?

Semi-Deductive Sermon Structure

One form of deductive movement that also has some similarities to the inductive structure is the subject-completed form. This form is probably the most common form used by preachers today. The subject-completed form is not a purely deductive form since the complete central thought is not given at the beginning of the sermon. It is similar to an inductive sermon in that only the subject is given in the introduction. That subject is then explored through multiple complements. Each of the main points gives part of the central idea. The listener is not given the complete central idea until the last point. It is similar to a deductive sermon in that each of the main points links back to the subject and not to the preceding point. And each point relates to the main idea in the same way. Consequently, this sermon form has a deductive feel to it.

The subject-completed sermon form is the workhorse form for most topical expository sermons and often for single text expository sermons. Many preachers use this form exclusively. On any given Sunday the majority of sermons preached may make use of this semi-deductive form.

The form is easily spotted when a preacher announces, for example, that he is speaking on the five keys to a happy marriage. The subject "how to have a happy marriage" is expressed in the introduction, and the five keys constitute the body of the sermon. Tension is maintained because the listener does not have the full answer to the question of how to have a happy marriage until the last major point of the sermon (and who would want to have only four keys to a happy marriage?).

The outline might look something like this:

"How to Have a Happy Marriage"

1. Key 1
2. Key 2
3. Key 3
4. Key 4
5. Key 5

The weakness of this form is that it does not always flow well from the text. After all, not every text comes complete with five principles or three keys or four benefits—most do not. The logic of a particular text does not often fit well into three or four parallel thoughts. Sometimes the text must be forced to fit into the mold of this form. But when it works, it is very effective. Its strengths are clarity of thought and the ability to communicate information well.

Parallel Logic

Both the deductive sermon form and the subject-completed form employ parallel logic. The main points are written in parallel form and each main point relates back to the subject in the same way. The sequence of the main points is not critical and can often be rearranged without any loss of movement. Transitions in subject-completed forms are often enumeration: "The third reason . . ." This kind of structure works well with a text that breaks down easily into parallel points. However, not every text is conducive to this kind of structure.

Forming Subject-Completed Sermons

How do we form subject-completed sermons? Look for passages with lists or which are capable of being formulated into a list. Is there a series of benefits listed? Are there three keys for effective prayer? Does the passage list four reasons not to worry? The subject-completed form works especially well with topical sermons. Since topical sermons have almost unlimited flexibility in choosing content, it is relatively easy to identify three, four, or five parallel thoughts for a topical sermon.

The subject-completed form is seen in this sermon by William E. Sangster. (I have supplied the subject and complement.)

"He Dies. He Must Die."

Sermon on Luke 24:26

Subject: Why it was necessary for Jesus Christ to be crucified

Complement: Because only a crucified Savior could reveal our sins, save us from our sins, and meet us in our agony.

  I. Jesus Christ had to be crucified because only a crucified Savior could reveal our sins.
 II. Jesus Christ had to be crucified because only a crucified Savior could save us from our sins.
III. Jesus Christ had to be crucified because only a crucified Savior could meet us in our agony.[5]

This sermon gives three reasons why it was necessary for Christ to be crucified. It is a multiple complement sermon. No-

tice that the order of the second and third points could easily
be switched.

Inductive Sermon Structure

The movement in the inductive sermon is from the particulars
to the general conclusions. Inductive preaching "begins with the
particulars of human experience and moves toward the often
surprising conclusions of the gospel."[6] In the inductive sermon
everything leads toward the statement of the central idea.

The introduction gives only the subject and the first main point
of the sermon. The complement is revealed as the sermon progresses. The full central idea is not revealed until near the end of
the sermon. This creates a sense of ambiguity and uncertainty as to
how the issue raised in the introduction will be resolved. Questions
are raised in the beginning and not answered until the end.

In inductive movement the main points in the sermon each link
to the preceding point. The transitions then are very important.
They show the logical connection between the successive points.
The inductive sermon is not concerned with parallel points. It
is concerned with the sequence of thoughts.

There are numerous advantages to the inductive form. The
inductive form is good for maintaining interest. Questions are
raised from the very beginning. Like a good story, the inductive form can capture our attention. The inductive form also
requires a greater degree of participation from the listener. The
inductive form is more of a conversation than a presentation; it
is more of a dialogue than a monologue since it seeks to begin
with the concerns of the listener. The listener is invited into the
sermon process. Since the full idea is not given until the end of
the sermon, inductive forms are especially valuable when dealing with hostile audiences. And induction may be the best form
for communicating with contemporary audiences. Calvin Miller
makes the bold claim that in our day induction "is not merely
a means of preaching the gospel—it is *the* means."[7]

A weakness of the inductive form may be that it is not always
as well suited as the deductive form for communicating the
content and information of the Scriptures.

Nathan's story to King David in 2 Samuel 12 is a great example of inductive movement. Nathan begins by telling David a story about a poor man and a lamb (vv. 1–4), he allows David to respond to the story (vv. 5–6), but the complete idea is not revealed until the dramatic indictment in verse 7: "You are the man!" Nathan then goes on to apply that indictment to David in deductive fashion. David then responds in repentance. Now imagine that Nathan had chosen a more deductive approach. Instead of a story, he could have begun with a statement of David's sin and then listed four consequences of that sin. Would David have still responded with repentance? Perhaps, but there is no doubt that the inductive approach was powerful and effective.

Two other examples of inductive movement are Stephen's speech in Acts 7 and Paul's sermon in Athens in Acts 17. In Stephen's address he is confronting a hostile audience. His speech begins in verse 2, but he doesn't get to the full statement of his idea until verses 51–53. Paul, as we have seen, begins with the Athenian listeners (their altar, their poets) before coming to a call to repentance and faith.

Sequential Logic

Rather than the parallel logic of deductive movement, inductive sermons use sequential logic.[8] Each main point is related to the previous main point. A logic of contrast, causation, and result is often used. With this kind of logic, the order cannot be easily altered. The use of sequence is one of the great advantages of the inductive form; it allows us to follow the twists and turns of the text in our presentation.

How Do We Form Inductive Sermons?

An inductive sermon may flow like this: begin with the particulars of the listener. The inductive sermon may start with a statement about the circumstance of the world in which we live. It may identify a sin or a difficult circumstance or struggle. The inductive sermon will usually begin with the need of the listener. As we have seen in chapter 2, this is what Paul Scott Wilson labels "trouble"[9] and Bryan Chapell calls the "Fallen Condition Focus."[10]

The first point of a sermon on Ephesians 1:7–10, which speaks of redemption and the forgiveness of sin, might go like this: "Sin is our problem. It is our great dilemma, our greatest predicament." The sermon begins with the listener and their greatest need before it turns to the solution, redemption and forgiveness.

The sermon then explores that situation. Lowry suggests that the ambiguity introduced in the first movement is complicated in the second movement.[11] It is worse than we thought. Our best efforts to resolve this problem fail. Often a problem/solution sermon will explore possible solutions that ultimately fail.

Occasionally, while my wife and I are watching a murder mystery on TV, the mystery seems to be solved halfway through the show. "It's too early," we say. And we are almost always right. The obvious solution turns out to be a dead end—it gets messier before it gets better. The inductive sermon will tend to complicate the problem before it solves it.

The sermon then moves toward the resolution of the situation in the gospel. This is Wilson's "grace"[12] and Chapell's "redemptive approach."[13] The truth of the gospel is brought to bear on the issue raised in the beginning. It is in this portion of the sermon that the full idea of the sermon is presented.

Finally, the sermon shows the result or consequence of applying the gospel to the situation. Here is what happens because of the central idea. The last point in an inductive sermon may often have the words "result" or "consequence" in it.

Of course, not every inductive sermon will follow that pattern. The inductive sermon is capable of enormous variety. Often an inductive sermon simply follows the flow of thought in the text. Since much of the Scripture comes to us in inductive form, a sermon that patterns itself on the form of the text will often be inductive. The narrative form is almost always inductive in its approach.

In forming an inductive sermon, our thinking might go like this: "In communicating this idea, the first thing I need to say is . . . The second thing is . . ." and so on.

Inductive/Deductive Sermon Structure

One more form to consider is the combination of inductive and deductive forms. In this sermon structure the sermon progresses in its initial movement in inductive fashion, coming to a statement of the central idea in the second or third main point. Once the central idea is given, the sermon must then proceed deductively. It will seek to explain, prove, or apply the central idea.[14] In my experience the most common use of this form ends by applying the sermon idea.

I recently preached an inductive/deductive sermon on finances from the book of Proverbs. I began by introducing my subject. I proceeded inductively through the first point to the statement of my homiletical idea: "We are to honor God with our finances." The rest of the sermon dealt deductively with the question, "What does it mean to honor God with our finances?" by looking at various verses from Proverbs.

A Case Study—Deductive and Inductive Structure

Stephen F. Olford developed the following Mother's Day sermon on 2 Timothy 1:1–5; 3:12–17.

"Faith of Our Mothers"
I. A Mother's Faith Is Convictional
  A. It is a faith which is Scripturally sound
  B. It is a faith which is savingly pure
II. A Mother's Faith Is Communicable
  A. Faith is communicated by personal education
  B. Faith is communicated by practical demonstration
III. A Mother's Faith Is Commendable
  A. The lasting influence of a mother's faith
  B. The lasting relevance of a mother's faith[15]

This well-structured sermon lists a number of particulars about a mother's faith. The logic and wording are all parallel. It is an example of a subject-completed form. It answers the question, What is a mother's faith like?

But we could design a sermon on this same passage using a more inductive approach. The homiletical idea could be stated like this: "The primary task of a mother is to communicate her faith to her children." To communicate this idea a number of tasks would have to be accomplished. The sermon task list might look like this:

a. show how communicating the faith must be a priority for a mother
b. start with the goal—raising a Timothy
c. explain what it means for a mother to communicate her faith
d. identify the obstacles to communicating your faith (i.e., single parent, working moms, husbands who do not share the mother's faith)
e. clearly explain why a mother must first have a sincere faith

These thoughts do not easily form into a deductive sermon outline with parallel wording and ideas. They can, however, be shaped in an inductive, conversational form:

d. You probably do not have an ideal circumstance. It is difficult being a mother.
b. Yet you can raise children of faith!
e. Raising children of faith starts with a sincere faith of your own.
c. But that's not enough; you have to pass on your faith to your children.
a. So, what must you do? Make communicating your faith to your children a priority.

This outline makes no attempt at parallel logic or wording, but follows the normal twists and turns of everyday language and thought. Instead of making a number of statements about a mother's faith, this sermon really tells one thing: you need to make communicating your faith to your children a priority. Each step in the sermon contributed to that one idea.

The inductive approach to preaching is not always easy (it seldom is). It will require hours of wrestling with the text and the sermon. Often the finished outline is less than perfect, but that's okay—perfection is not required! Similarly, the rewards of the inductive form can be a sermon which better fits the inductive shape of the text and the inductive life of the listeners.

Choosing a Form

At some point in the sermon process, a commitment needs to be made to a specific sermon form. This commitment should not be made prematurely, but it does need to be made. You will want to choose the kind of movement you will use. You will consider the basic ways in which sermons can be formed. You might sketch out a number of different sermon designs. And finally you will choose the form that will be best for this Sunday's sermon.

In order to have a greater variety in your preaching design, it is helpful to intentionally choose different forms. Look for texts that can be formed using the subject-completed form, experiment with inductive and inductive/deductive forms. Try preaching a purely deductive sermon. I am in the habit of naming the form I use at the top of my sermon manuscript. This helps me to see if I am varying my form week by week (and too often I do not).

It is probable that you will feel most comfortable with a certain sermon form. For many that is the subject-completed form. I am most comfortable with an inductive or inductive/deductive form. But all of us should strive to have some variety in the forms that we use.

10

PREACHING THE
NARRATIVE GENRE

From Text to Focus	From Focus to Form	Developing the Sermon	Delivering the Sermon

A sermon idea may take the form of a narrative of events, persons, actions, and words. The distinguishing feature of this form is that the idea is embodied in a structure of events and persons, rather than in a structure of verbal generalizations.

H. Grady Davis, *Design for Preaching*

All of us preach from narrative texts. Since the narrative genre is the most common form in the Bible, preaching from narrative forms is almost unavoidable. An important homiletical question then is How is preaching the narrative genre different from preaching other genres? In this chapter we will explore different ways to form narrative sermons.

Literary Form and Sermon Form

From the work of literary criticism and form criticism has come an increasing awareness that the literary form (or genre) is part of the meaning of the text. Seeing the connection between form and content is essential to understanding a text's meaning. The form is part of the meaning. It follows then that the form of the text should affect the form of the sermon. There needs to be a relationship between literary form and homiletical form.

There is no consensus across the board on the exact designation of the various genres in Scripture. But as mentioned earlier, some of the major genres are narrative, prophecy, wisdom, psalm, gospel, epistle, and apocalypse.[1] Calvin Miller is helpful to preachers when he suggests three broad categories of genre: precept, narrative, and poetry.[2]

This is not to suggest that the form of the sermon should be identical to the form of the text. A sermon on a parable does not have to be a parable. Rather the form of the sermon should *reflect* the form of the text. Or put differently, the form of the text should *influence* the form of the sermon. We should allow the rhetorical impact of the textual form to be translated into the sermon as much as possible. Thomas Long clarifies what our goal should be: "The preacher's task . . . is not to replicate the text but to regenerate the impact of some portion of that text."[3] Such observations lead us to conclude that there is an increasing awareness among homileticians that literary form should affect sermon form.

Narrative

The need for the form of the text to influence the form of the sermon applies to each of the genres. But it is particularly with the narrative genre that literary form and sermon form most clearly intersect. Narrative is the predominate genre of the Bible. Narrative is particularly appropriate as a genre of Scripture because Christianity itself is the story of redemption. God acted in history. The Bible is the story of God and of God's acts in history. Sidney Greidanus states that "of all the biblical genres of literature, narrative may be described as the central, foundational, and all-encompassing genre of the Bible."[4] Thomas Long notes that "narrative is the dominant form of choice for biblical writers."[5] Since we will encounter narrative so often in our preaching journey, we want to focus on preaching the narrative genre in this chapter.[6]

Narrative Sermons

More than any other genre, narrative form should influence the pattern of our preaching. In almost every case a sermon on a passage in the narrative genre should reflect that genre in its form. A narrative text cries out for a narrative sermon design. Haddon Robinson reminds us, for instance, that "the parable of the prodigal son should not be reduced to 'four lessons we learn about God's love.'"[7] Jesus told a parable and our sermon form should reflect that.

So one of the challenges of sermon design is how to structure sermons for the narrative genre. We will not approach sermons on narrative texts in just the same way we approach nonnarrative texts.

What Is Narrative?

Before we consider preparing and preaching narrative sermons, we should discuss what a narrative is. A narrative is a story. It consists of a connected chain of events that leads to a conclusion.[8] A narrative has a beginning, which presents a problem, some unresolved situation. At the beginning of any story there is always some complication or struggle. This creates tension. At the beginning of the television crime series *CSI: Crime Scene Investigation*, someone invariably has been murdered. (It's only a surprise on *CSI* when someone doesn't die!) The murder creates a problem. Who did it? And how did he or she do it? How will the investigators identify the perpetrator? The beginning of any story starts with a problem.

The middle portion of the story bridges the gap between the problem and the resolution. It often complicates the problem or further defines it. In *CSI* the investigators follow up leads, interrogate suspects, and process evidence. Sometimes their leads are dead ends, witnesses may be uncooperative, or someone else may die. Typically, it gets messier before it becomes clearer. So the middle portion of a narrative expands upon the problem without resolving the conflict.

The end section is the resolution or denouement of the story. Here the problem is resolved, and the question is answered often in a rather unexpected way. Most often in the *CSI* television show the investigators get their man. Through some scientific technique they are able to ascertain who committed the crime. And often it is not who we expect. And, even in the few times when they cannot arrest the guilty party, there is some sense of resolution such as "Life isn't always fair," or "We'll get him in the end." Any good story has a conclusion, which resolves the conflict. Television shows that end with "to be continued" are inherently unsatisfying. Why? It is because there is no conclusion; the tension raised early in the show is not resolved. You have to wait until the following week to find out how it turns out. Thus goes the story.

Narrative is story: it has a beginning, middle, and an end. But narrative is not just story—it is story told for a purpose. Long reminds us that narrative functions to make a claim about life.[9] The writer had a purpose in writing this particular passage. Even the *CSI* show, whose purpose may be to entertain and sell advertising, makes a claim about life. *CSI* makes the claim that "the evidence will find you out in the end" or "right triumphs over wrong." So when we encounter a narrative portion of Scripture, we ask, Why is this passage here? What is its purpose in the book? What is its purpose in the larger context of Scripture? Finding the claim about life in a biblical narrative may open the door to the sermon design.

The Characteristics of Narrative Preaching

The term *narrative preaching* is sometimes used to refer to the inner logic and movement of a sermon regardless of the literary genre. Eugene Lowry defines a narrative sermon as "any sermon in which the arrangement of ideas takes the form of a plot involving a strategic delay of the preacher's meaning."[10] Such a broad use of the term *narrative* is all but indistinguishable from inductive preaching. Indeed narrative preaching could be considered a form of inductive preaching. For Lowry, a sermon on any genre can be a "narrative sermon."

But here I am using the term *narrative preaching* more narrowly to refer to a sermon whose design evidences the characteristics of story and is an exposition of a text with the attributes of story. A narrative sermon is structured as a plot (rather than an outline) and is based on a text which has a plot. When preaching on a text that is narrative (structured as a story) in form, it is most often appropriate to design a sermon that reflects the narrative form of the passage.

What distinguishes the narrative sermon from other forms is its structure. Narrative sermons "think more" in terms of plot than outline. As quoted in this chapter's epigraph, H. Grady Davis says that "the distinguishing feature of [the narrative] form is that the idea is embodied in a structure of events and persons, rather than in a structure of verbal generalizations."[11] The narrative sermon is storylike in its development, with a beginning, middle, and an ending. Miller contends that the narrative sermon does not contain stories but is a story (in its structure).[12]

Thus, like a story the narrative sermon will delay the full expression of the central idea until the end or near the end of the sermon. In that sense the narrative sermon has an overall inductive design.

The Advantages of the Narrative Sermon

There are numerous advantages to the narrative sermon. One obvious advantage is that narrative is the form of the text. "By using the same form as the text," Greidanus explains, "one acknowledges the significance of the biblical form and is less likely to distort the text."[13] As suggested earlier, the literary form is part of the meaning of the text. We are most faithful to that meaning when we bring the form across our homiletical bridge. Narrative also creates interest. Everyone likes a story, especially a good story. Stories hold our attention in ways that lectures cannot. The narrative sermon gains our interest through its story-like quality. We may know that in the end of a murder mystery the hero will get his man, but the story genre demands that we listen to find out exactly how and who the murderer is.

The narrative form encourages involvement. It asks the listener to participate in a journey. The listener is invited to walk alongside the characters of the story. We usually identify with one of the characters. Ronald Allen reminds us that through story "the ancient listener or reader encountered the text not by having it 'explained' but by entering its world."[14]

Narrative is also effective because we live in a storied world. Preachers compete with television and movies for people's attention. Even the evening news is often presented in a story form. So narrative form is an important biblical tool for communicating to contemporary culture.

Designing Narrative Sermons

The process of designing narrative sermons is similar to the basic sermon design process. And yet there are differences. In designing the narrative sermon, we must think in terms of plot, not outline. The full meaning must be delayed until the end. There needs to be a beginning, middle, and conclusion. To design a narrative sermon, we must enter the world of narrativity and think in narrative terms. The sermon design process will need to be modified accordingly.

Step 1: Begin with the Sermon Focus

As in the basic sermon design process, begin with the focus: the homiletical idea and the purpose of the sermon. Like all other forms of literature, the narrative genre contains a central idea and a purpose. The first task is to determine the exegetical idea of the passage. Paul Borden and Steven D. Mathewson have identified eleven exegetical elements in determining the idea of a narrative portion: design, scenes, characters, action, dialogue, language, narration, plot, tone, rhetorical structures, and context.[15] Each of these elements contributes to the exegetical understanding of the passage. After considering these exegetical elements, write out a one-sentence description of each scene in the narrative. From those statements, formulate the exegetical idea. The homiletical idea will then flow from the exegetical idea as you consider it in relation to your contemporary audience.[16]

Next we need to determine the purpose. Stories are not aimless. The author had a reason for writing what he wrote. We determine the purpose of the author by asking: Why did the author write this? What was his purpose? What is his claim about life? We determine the purpose for our sermon by asking: What do I want to accomplish through this sermon? What do I want the listener to do? What is the claim that this sermon will make on the listener?

Step 2: Do a Plot Analysis

The plot is the storyline, including the twists and turns of the biblical story, plus the complications, conflicts, and ultimate resolution. Write out the plot of the narrative text, including the beginning, middle, and end. Write out a brief summary of each section or scene. You will have already done some of this in your exegetical work and in determining the homiletical idea. This is the time to revisit that work. Take time to consider the story in light of the larger context of the book in which it is found and in the context of Scripture as a whole. The plot of your sermon will likely (though not always) follow the contours of the plot of the text. The major thought or movements of the sermon and the sequence may simply follow the flow of the text.

Step 3: Notice Any Literary Devices or Features

Narrative fulfills its purpose by making use of various rhetorical devices. One such device is characterization. Characterization refers to the way in which key characters are developed in the plot. From what perspective does the passage present the characters in the story? What does the passage emphasize about the characters? Who is the protagonist? Detail is important. Robert Alter says, "When a particular descriptive detail is mentioned—Esau's ruddiness and hairiness, Rachel's beauty, King Eglon's obesity—we should be alert for consequences, immediate or eventual, either in plot or theme."[17] Other rhetorical devices include repetition, allusion, direct discourse, inclusion, and chiasm.[18] Inclusion occurs when a section begins and ends with the same sentence or phrase. Chiasm is a form of parallelism in which the central element is the focal point. The pattern may look something like this:

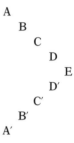

Reader identification is another feature to look for in narrative literature. With whom in the story does the author intend his reader to identify? For a recent sermon from Exodus 2, I had to determine whether the author intended the reader to identify with Moses or the people of Israel. The answer to that question was essential for designing the sermon.

These rhetorical devices offer cues for the meaning of the text and, at times, to the design for the sermon. Which of the above ought to influence the structure of your sermon? What can you bring across the homiletical bridge into your sermon?

Step 4: Do an Audience Analysis

A narrative is intended to be told to an audience. The author of the narrative had an intended audience. Your audience will be somewhat different. Ask yourself questions about the audience: What in this story needs to be explained to the modern listener? What objections might they raise? How can they apply the truth of this narrative to their lives? How can you attain the same effect for your audience as the original author did for his?

Step 5: Complete a Sermon Task List

As in the basic sermon design process, you will want to create a task list of what must be said and done in communicating this text. What does this sermon need to say and do to accomplish its purpose for this audience? What key events in the narrative need to be highlighted? In brainstorming for your task list, you will explore the biblical narrative and the contemporary audience. Your task list may include contemporary stories that need to be told. When you are done you will have a list of ideas, many of which will be included in your final sermon design.

Step 6: Replot the Text in Terms of the Sermon

Start with determining the type of narrative form you will use. Various stock narrative structures are available. Below I will suggest a number of possible designs. Knowing that there are only so many ways to design a narrative sermon helps us in the design process.

Once we have determined the basic narrative approach we will take, we need to think of sequence. Bring together the threads from your sermon task list and the narrative form that you will use and replot the text in terms of your homiletical idea and purpose. To replot is to take the plot of the biblical story and (in light of your homiletical idea, purpose, and the rhetorical situation) create a sermon plot that will say and do for your audience what the biblical story said and did for its audience. You may try several possible plot sequences before finding one that works. It will be a creative retelling of the biblical story. This will be your sermon structure.

Approaches to Narrative Sermons

In step 6 for designing narrative sermons, we determine the type of narrative sermon we will use. Although often the sermon form will arise naturally from the text, it is helpful to be aware of some basic ways in which your sermon may be developed. Here are some ways in which a narrative sermon might progress.

Allow the Movement of the Sermon to Follow the Movement of the Text

This is perhaps the most commonly used form for narrative preaching. Eugene Lowry calls this form "running the story."[19]

It is my normal approach to narrative texts. In this approach the story, application, and contemporary examples are all interwoven throughout the sermon. The plot of the sermon follows the plot of the text. In essence the text gives you your outline. Contemporary application is included throughout. Repetition of this form is not boring since the story told from sermon to sermon, week to week, is always different.

Here is an example of a narrative structure from an Easter sermon on Matthew 28:1–10:

1. We are all skeptics. Like the women who went to the tomb, we come to Easter with our questions and doubts.
2. So God gives us an empty tomb. Call it exhibit 1: the empty tomb.
3. But an empty tomb by itself is never enough. So God gives us a living Jesus. That's exhibit 2: the appearances of Jesus.
4. How should we respond? Like the women on Easter morning, we worship Him.
5. And like the women, we respond in the obedience of faith.

This sermon structure followed the basic flow of the text. Notice that each point is written with a contemporary perspective. Although the main points refer back to the biblical story, they retain a contemporary perspective ("God gives *us* an empty tomb"). I thought of using a past tense structure (i.e., "the women were skeptics . . .") but came to the conclusion that a present tense perspective was more direct and relevant.

After stating the point, each point was developed by telling the biblical story and exploring contemporary applications of that truth. Each section was then concluded with a restatement of the main point.

Tell the Biblical Story

Telling the biblical story is what John Holbert calls "pure narrative."[20] The narrative sermon is a creative contemporizing of the biblical story. According to Holbert, it has no introduction or conclusion ("the story's introduction is the sermon's introduction; the story's conclusion is the sermon's conclusion"[21]); it consists only of the story told with contemporary language. To use this form well requires a significant ability in storytelling.

Tell the Biblical Story and Then Tell a Contemporary Story or Stories

The preacher may tell the biblical story and end by sharing a personal story or stories that mirror the focus of the biblical story. The contemporary stories serve as an application of the biblical story. Miller gives us an example of this in his sermon on Genesis 32.

"Encounter at Jabbok"

1. Jacob wrestles with God at the river Jabbok.
   (Miller shares the story in a humorous and contemporary fashion.)
2. Three contemporary stories of wrestling with God.[22]
   (Miller shares three personal stories of times when he wrestled with God.)

Present a Problem Using a Contemporary Story and Then Present the Biblical Story as the Solution

Holbert calls a sermon that begins with a contemporary story, tells the biblical story, and then ends with a contemporary story or image a "frame narrative."[23] In a sermon on Luke 15:1–7, Michael Quicke told a story about the need for rescue, using a story of the dramatic rescue of trapped miners. He then retold the biblical story, told his own story of spiritual rescue, and concluded with the listener's need for rescue.[24]

Use a Dramatic Monologue

Dramatic monologue as a sermon form is also called a first person narrative. In this sermon form the preacher tells the story from the perspective of one of the characters. This can be an effective form if done well and not too often. Robinson suggests the following guidelines.[25]

- Choose the character, the event, or the story to preach.
- Do research on the character.

- Do research on the setting.
- Be sure that your portrayal of the character is tied to the text. The meaning and function of the text should come through the character.
- Develop a plot. The plot can follow the movement of the biblical story, make use of a flashback structure that begins with the conclusion, or some other variation.

In a recent Christmas sermon on Luke 1:26–38, I took the perspective of the angel Gabriel. I told Mary's story through Gabriel's words. The sermon plot looked like this:

1. Mary was an ordinary young girl.
2. But my message to her was extraordinary. It was the message of a savior.
3. That wasn't all: it was the message of a king.
4. But Mary saw a problem: she was a virgin. So I told her it would be a supernatural birth.
5. Now let me tell you how Mary responded. She responded in the obedience of faith.

A Good Story

Narrative forms are effective because everyone is interested in a good story. At a recent luncheon for a departing employee at my church, a certain topic was brought up. Someone immediately said, "I have a story about that . . ." Instantly everyone was listening. We all love a story.

However we do it, narrative texts cry out to be preached in a narrative form. So the next time you confront a narrative text, try not to cram it into the mold of your usual form—allow the form of the text to shine through. Make your sermon a narrative sermon.

11

EXPANDING THE
SERMON FORM

From Text to Focus	From Focus to Form	Developing the Sermon	Delivering the Sermon

A preacher must learn to handle words and apply them with enchantment and conviction and passion. I am convinced that most preachers cannot arrive at a professional use of rhetoric without a love of words. And the power of oratory must be given the kind of advantage that only comes with writing.

Calvin Miller, *Preaching: The Art of Narrative Exposition*

A basic sermon form is not a sermon. As a skeleton is not a body, so the sermon form, whether narrative or deductive or inductive, needs to be developed. The skeleton needs flesh and muscle. Somehow the sermon must be expanded. Every preacher does it—but what is it that we do? What is the process that will take us from basic design to sermon? In this chapter we want to consider different ways of expanding the initial sermon structure into a complete sermon. This is the third phase of the sermon process: developing the sermon.

The result of the first phase of sermon preparation is the sermon focus: a clearly written homiletical idea and sermon purpose. At the end of the second phase, we should have a basic sermon form: a series of preachable ideas in a particular sequence. This third phase should yield a sermon manuscript or at least a fully developed outline.

Developing a main point is a matter of shaping the material we have before us. This phase of the sermon process assumes we have done the hard work of study and reflection and sermon design and therefore have material to shape. David Buttrick chides that if we don't have enough material to shape, then the thinking-through process is incomplete.[1]

But even when we have material before us—from our study of the text, our reflection on the audience, and our development of a basic design—it is not always easy to see the way to develop the sermon design. Every preacher has experienced the frustration of staring at a blank sheet of paper or a blinking cursor on a blank computer screen. Call it writer's block or sermonic gridlock: sometimes the path is not clear. What is needed is a way that will allow the main points to grow and develop out of the preaching passage. In other words, we need a process. Process is the path toward creative thought. Process gives us the structure that will enable us to think through the sermon development. The following four steps can help the preacher find the way through the creative process of developing the sermon form.

Step 1: Do a Homiletic Analysis for Each Main Point

A homiletic analysis[2] takes the work of exegesis (exegesis of the text and exegesis of the audience/culture) and considers it from a homiletic perspective. By the time we arrive at a basic structure, we should have before us pages of notes, thoughts, and illustration ideas. These are the creative material and observations that may or may not become part of the sermon. A homiletic analysis will help you to identify the material that needs to be shaped in the development of the main points. A homiletic analysis should be done for each main point. It consists of five parts.

The Opening Statement

First, the homiletic analysis begins with writing out the opening statement for a main point. This, of course, has been developed in rough form in the basic sermon design. The opening statement should be expressed in a complete sentence and should express a single thought. Keep it simple. Statements that express multiple thoughts create confusion in oral communication. If the opening statement is not clear to us, then we should not proceed. The process of development cannot move ahead until each of the main points can be written succinctly and clearly.

Biblical Support

Second, we need to take time to consider the biblical support for each main point. This will include the verse or verses in the text at hand as well as any related Scriptures. The Scripture should support each main thought. We do not need to use each of the related Scriptures in the final sermon draft. In fact, we will be cautious of the overuse of biblical cross-references. But it is important that the main point be well grounded in the Bible.

Theology

Third, write out the theological concern of the point. This is the theology that flows from the passage upon which the point is based. Each main point should be making some theological claim about God or life or both. What is the view of God expressed in this point? Here we bring in our systematic theology. Preaching is applied theology.

Congregational Objections

Fourth, identify any congregational objections to the point under consideration. If your listeners could stand and raise objections during your sermon, what objections might they voice concerning this point? Try to think of the sermon from the listeners' perspectives. What might listeners say they don't understand? What statements might they question in terms of validity? Does the listener "buy" what you are saying? This is an important way of inviting the listener into the sermon design process. If we think carefully, we can identify potential congregational objections to the main point with which we are working. The purpose of identifying objections, of course, is to answer those objections in the development of the point. There will not always be objections, but often there will be.

Images, Examples, and Illustrations

Finally, write out any initial ideas of images, examples, or illustrations that can help you communicate this idea. In your study you may have scribbled down various possibilities. Now is the time to brainstorm a bit. Think about the text, your audience, and life. Images are word pictures, examples are a slice of life, and illustrations have the character of story (beginning, middle, and end). These images, examples, and illustrations will flow from the biblical text but will ordinarily be located in contemporary culture and time.

Sometimes it is helpful to fill out a worksheet for a homiletical analysis of a main point, with its five parts as shown below.

Homiletic Analysis of a Main Point

Opening Statement:

Biblical Support:

Theology:

Congregational Objections:

Images, Examples, Illustrations:

Doing a homiletic analysis allows us to identify the material we will shape in developing each main point. This analysis helps us overcome the gridlock of the blank sheet of paper or computer screen. Once we have completed a homiletic analysis for each main point, we are ready to move ahead.

Step 2: Write a Beginning Draft

Once the homiletic analysis is completed, we are ready to write a beginning draft of the sermon. The discipline of writing a draft for each main point is essential. The process of writing forces us to think through the development of the point and helps us to begin to shape the content for the point. This draft will make use of the material identified in our study and the homiletic analysis. In this step we will begin the process of shaping the material into oral form.

Three Parts of a Draft

The draft of each point will consist of an opening (the statement of the main point), several developmental paragraphs, and a closing statement (a restatement of the main point).

THE OPENING STATEMENT

Since the opening statement has already been clearly formulated, this step only involves writing down the main point. Later, we will discuss expanding the opening statement through restatement.

Example of the Opening of a Main Point

Sermon on Romans 6
"We begin with a question: Shall we go on sinning?"

THE DEVELOPMENT

The opening statement is followed by several developmental paragraphs. Rather than subpoints, it is better to think of the *development* of the main point. The development will consist of explanation, application, proof, or a response to a congregational objection. The developmental paragraphs make use of the images, examples, and illustrations developed in our homiletical analysis. The developmental systems of a main point should function to create one thought in the mind of the listener. Every main point will have two or three or at the most four developmental paragraphs. Each main point will ordinarily be approximately four to five minutes long. When the main point is longer, the listener's mind will probably wander. When it is shorter, the point may not be fully developed.

One of the developmental paragraphs may be a response to a perceived congregational objection. Normally, the response to objections should come early in the development of the point so we may conclude with a positive statement of the point.

The development of the point should be designed to create some change in the thinking of the listener. If some significant change is not achieved, then the point was unnecessary. So each point will challenge the listener to think differently in some significant way. Progress should be made; the point needs to develop!

THE CLOSE

Each main point needs to close. Just as a narrative needs an ending, so your thought needs closure. This can be accomplished in one of two ways. First, closure can be indicated by restatement of the opening statement at the end of the point. Restating the point has the effect of framing the point in the consciousness of the listener. It brings a sense of completeness. Buttrick makes the sweeping statement that closure always involves a return to the idea of the opening statement.[3] So at the end of a main point, we may restate the main idea.

Here is an example of closure through restatement taken from one main point for a sermon on Micah 5.

Opening statement: Here is the problem: this is an insecure world.

Closing statement: We live in an insecure world.

Restating the opening statement at the end of the point indicates to the listener that that thought is concluded. The way is now prepared for the opening statement of the next main point.

A second way closure can be indicated is through the use of transitions between points. Thomas Long informs us that transitions "provide closure for the preceding segment of the sermon, thus reassuring the hearers that they are on the right track."[4] For instance, the transition "Not only . . . but (also) . . ." gives closure to the preceding thought and prepares the way for the next thought.

Failure to bring closure to a point is one reason a listener can get lost in following the progress of the sermon. You may have moved on to your next thought while your listener is still stuck back in the preceding one! However we do it, we need to communicate that one main point has come to an end so that the listener can prepare for a new thought.

The Structure of Development

The classic approach to sermon development is to create parallel subpoints. Bryan Chapell explains that "subpoints organize and develop the thought of a main point. They should exhibit parallelism, proportion, and progression; each should relate to the main point in a similar fashion."[5]

Subpointing done as Chapell suggests can look like this:

Main Point	*Because Jesus provides the only hope of salvation,* we must present Christ despite our difficulties.
Subpoints	1. In circumstantial difficulties 2. In relational difficulties 3. In spiritual difficulties[6]

Certainly this kind of outline can work. Yet must a sermon be developed in this way? Does every subpoint in a sermon have to be developed in parallel thoughts, having the same relationship to the main point? And if we do outline the main point with parallel subpoints, does each subpoint then itself require development (explanation, application, and illustration)? If so, each subpoint will tend to stand alone. The main point will not register as one thought but as two or three separate thoughts.

An outline of this kind may be appropriate for certain texts and in certain occasions, but two factors warn against the overuse of this kind of subpointing. First, it is evident that the Scriptures do not come to us with this kind of strict logical presentation.

Rather, the Bible comes to us with epistle, with story, with digressions, with all the twists and turns of which human speech is capable. We need an approach to structure that allows us to reflect the structure of Scripture.

And second, effective oral communication does not require this kind of parallel structure. We don't talk that way in normal conversation, and it is not necessary to talk that way in public discourse.

In any case, subpoints should not be emphasized. David Larsen argues that we should intentionally de-emphasize the statement of subpoints.[7] I recently listened to a sermon that had several main points and numerous subpoints (and maybe sub-subpoints—I wasn't totally sure), all in parallel form. But I was lost most of the time; it was just too complicated to follow. It is enough for the listener to track the main thoughts.

A more flexible approach to the development of main points is needed. I prefer to think in terms of developmental paragraphs rather than subpoints. These developmental paragraphs do not need to be written in parallel form. Our development must be able to take into account the form of the text as well as the needs of the rhetorical situation.

Each developmental paragraph should move the point ahead in some significant way. This can happen through explanation, through proof, through application, through illustration, or through responding to some congregational objection.

Taking this approach to sermon development for each main point looks something like this:

Example of a Developmental Paragraph Structure

Opening
Development 1
Congregational Objection
Development 2
Illustration
Close

In preparing a sermon on Exodus 3:10–4:17, I structured the message around Moses's five objections to God's call. Part of the sermon went like this:

1. Excuse #1: I am inadequate.
   Development A: Moses was inadequate.
   Congregational Block: If we are honest, we all struggle
   with a sense of inadequacy.
   Development B: God responded to Moses's inadequacy.
   Illustration: J. Hudson Taylor quote
   Application to our inadequacy
   Close: That was Moses's first excuse: I am inadequate.

2. Excuse #2: I don't know enough.
   Development A: Moses's request was reasonable—he needed
   to know more.
   Development B: God's response to Moses: "I AM WHO I
   AM."
   Application to life
   Close: Moses didn't know enough.

3. Excuse #3: I might fail.
   Development A: Moses feared failure.
   Development B: God responded by demonstrating his
   power.
   Illustration: Story of missionary candidate
   Application to our fear of failure
   Close: Moses feared failure.

The structure in this sermon flowed from the structure of the
text: Moses's objections and God's responses.

Material for Writing Out the Beginning Draft

The following strategies can be used to explain, prove, apply,
or amplify the thought of your sermon.

RESTATEMENT

Restatement is expressing the same thought in different words.
Restatement in oral communication is a way of expressing emphasis. It should always occur in the opening statements but
may also be used for emphasis with key points in the development of the point. In general, key ideas should be restated for
emphasis.

EXPLANATION

We bring out the theology or meaning of a sermon point and the passage upon which it is based by explaining and defining. Explanation is a significant aspect of expository preaching. Nehemiah 8:8 states that the Levites "read from the Book of the Law of God, making it clear and giving the meaning so that the people could understand what was being read." Some sermons may be primarily explanatory, but all sermons should include some explanation.

FACTUAL INFORMATION

Sometimes statistics or other factual information can reinforce the thought of the sermon. Statistics can be used to explain or prove. Statistics should be used sparingly and, when they are used, it is best to use them early in the sermon.

QUOTATIONS

Use quotations only when they add something to the sermon. Quotations should never be more than a few sentences long or at the most a paragraph. Long quotations generally do not work well in oral communication. Don't use quotations just for the sake of quoting. There are two reasons to use quotations: the eloquence of the statement or the authority of the person making the statement.

NARRATION

Narration in essence is telling the biblical story. Tell it in as interesting and creative a way as possible. Or tell a contemporary story. One important way to use narration is to make use of dialogue. Preachers are storytellers. That is not all they are, but telling stories is an important part of the preaching task.

IMAGES, EXAMPLES, AND ILLUSTRATIONS

We have already begun to think of images, examples and illustrations under step 1. Now is the time to complete the brainstorming process and select which images, examples, or illustrations will find their way into this sermon. Each of these can be used in various ways to restate, explain, validate, or apply ideas. We live in an image-rich world. But that is not anything new. The Bible is rich with visual images. And preachers have always made use of illustration, example, and image.

Image is a word picture. Look for images in the text. Make use of the same images in the sermon. Usually you will want to work with the dominant image of the text. So, for instance, in a sermon on the parable of four soils, we may want to make use of agricultural images as much as possible. We will try to make use of vocabulary taken from the agricultural world.

Examples are cases in point. They tend to be static. They are a snapshot of life. Sometimes we will group a series of examples (most often three) to form one image in the mind of the listener. When I delivered the sermon on Exodus 3:10–4:17, mentioned just before, I gave three examples of our inadequacy:

- Maybe you have been asked to teach a children's class and felt inadequate.
- Or you were asked to lead a small group and you responded by saying, "Who am I?"
- Or you were asked to help with the youth group and came to the conclusion that you didn't have what it takes.

Notice that these examples are written in parallel form.

Illustrations have plot, which include some point of tension and resolution. We will probably not make use of illustration for each point but will seek to illustrate the most important points in the sermon. Thus we will make use of image, example, and illustration to develop a sermon point.

IMAGE GRID

I am indebted to Buttrick for the suggestion of using an image grid in the development process.[8] To create an image grid, I write out the words *image, example,* and *illustration* across the top of the page. On the left side I write a number for each main point. I then fill in the grid for each point. This helps me to achieve balance. I can easily see if I have two similar sounding illustrations too close to one another in the sermon. This may cause the points to become confused in the listener's mind. I will want examples and imagery for each point. I will probably not want an illustration for each point and certainly not more than one for each point. And I can easily see if I have illustrations for the key points. I can then make use of the material found in my image grid in writing my beginning draft.

Sermon point	Image	Example	Illustration
1.			
2.			
3.			

Once a draft is written, it will need to be refined and rewritten several times. But the written draft helps to clarify thinking and structure.

Deductive and Inductive Movement

Most often the development of a main point will be deductive in its movement. It will begin with a clear statement of the point and then proceeds to explain, prove, and/or apply that main thought. Deductive movement in the point can be used even when the overall movement of the sermon is inductive. For a variation on this approach, the main thought development could also be approached inductively. In this case the statement of the point is not given in the opening statement. Instead, the opening will probably consist of some form of question and the full statement of the point will occur toward the end of the development.

Step 3: Add Transitions

The movement from one main point to another demands some form of transition. In a book, bold headings are often used to help the reader transition from one thought to another. In an oral medium, verbal transitions mark the progress of thought.

A while back my wife and I were invited to dinner at the childhood home of our son's wife, Katie. As we traveled to their home, my son was in the backseat giving me direction at critical times. "Get on I-287 going north," he said. A little later he said, "Now take Route 202." Finally, Katie chimed in, "It's the third house on the left." Those directions served as transitions from one portion of our journey to the next. Without them we would have been hopelessly lost. Transitions are important.

Transitions help us in three ways. First, transitions can provide closure for the proceeding point. They tell us that the thought is complete. They inform the listener that one point is finished, and we are about to move on to the next thought.

Second, transitions show the logical connection between the main points. This function is especially important in inductive sermons, which progress sequentially, but is less important in deductive preaching since each main point relates back to the central idea in the same way.

Third, transitions anticipate the content of the next section. The listener needs to know not only where they have been but also some idea of where they are going. Good transitions give us a glimpse of the next main point.

Overall, transitions enable us to follow the progress of the thought. They keep the listener from getting lost in a maze of verbiage. Transitions make the sermon followable. "We are done with that thought and now we want to consider this thought." When people can't follow our preaching, we may need to spend more time developing the sermon's transitions.

Duane Litfin lists three types of transitions. First, additional transitions are transitions that let us know that something new is about to be added to what precedes. "Additional transitions are those which show one point building upon another."[9] They use words or phrases such as "in addition to . . ." or "furthermore . . ." or "now let's consider another idea . . ."

Second, inferential transitions let us know that some form of logical inference is being made. The point to come is somehow built upon the foundation of the previous point. Key words that signal inferential transitions include "therefore . . ." and "so, it follows from this that . . ."

Third, disjunctive transitions show a contrast between sermon points. The following are disjunctive transitions: "yet, even though . . ." or "but . . ." or "on the other hand . . ."

A fourth category of transitions that should be added is the often-used enumeration. "First, second, and third" may not be creative, but it is certainly clear. This type of transition is most often used in deductive and semi-deductive sermon forms. The danger that accompanies its overuse is predictability. In general, I try to find another form of transition when possible. But when giving a list of ideas, enumeration works well.

Sometimes I use a question as a way to transition from one thought to the next. It might look something like this: "Why is that (the preceding thought) so? Because . . ." For instance in a sermon on Ephesians 2:8–10, the first two points were "we are saved by grace" and "we are not saved by works." The third point raised the question, "Why is salvation by grace and not of works?" I then gave the answer—"so that no one can boast."

Transitions may be developed in two ways. The first way is to write out separate transitional statements. This is the traditional approach to transitions, and it is still very effective. A transitional statement may be as short as a single word ("but . . .") or may consist of a few sentences. Generally, shorter is better. Long or complicated transitions may not serve the sermon well.

A second way of designing transitions, proposed by Buttrick, is to make the closing statement of a point and opening statement of the next point work together as the transition.[10] Buttrick suggests that if the thoughts of a sermon are written in conversational language, separate transitional statements are unnecessary. In effect, the closing statement of the proceeding thought and the opening statement of the next main point together function as the transition.

The sequence of thought for a sermon from Micah 7:1–10 could be written as follows:

> We live in a world gone wrong.
> It is possible to live in such a world with confidence.
> God is the God who rescues us.
> Live with confidence in God.

These four main points need some kind of transitional statement between each section. They need some kind of verbal vehicle to travel from one thought to the next. But if they are rewritten in conversational language, no separate transitional statements are necessary. The connecting logic is contained in the combination of closing statement of one point and the opening statement of the following point.

We live in a world gone wrong.

And yet it is possible to live in such a world with confidence.

Why can we have such confidence? We can have such confidence because our God is the God who rescues us.

So, live with confidence in God.

The restatement of the main thought at the end of each point along with the statement of the next main point together serve as the transition. The key is to write out the points in conversational language. In writing our sermon draft and especially in writing transitions, we should write the way we speak. When we do that, one thought flows smoothly into the following thought and separate transitional statements may be unnecessary.

Step 4: Develop the Final Form

In this final stage of developing the sermon's finished form, we are concerned with language and image. We edit and polish the sermon's language. Whether the sermon is fully written out or not, working on word choice is important. We may not use all of the language we choose, but much of it will come back to us as we speak.

Opening Statement

The opening should now be written not as a single sentence but as a group of sentences. These sentences are not different statements but a restatement of the one idea. Restatement is not mere repetition but a creative rephrasing of the idea. Repetition says the same thing in the same words. Restatement says the same thing in different words. Repetition sounds, well, repetitious. Restatement highlights a point. Restatement in orality functions in the same way that italics function in a literary work. It proclaims, "This is important!"

Editing

A sermon is best written over a period of days. We write out a beginning draft. Then we return to the sermon draft to edit. We write and then rewrite and rewrite, always looking to say it a little bit better. We need to take time to wrestle with wording and illustrations and ideas. Allowing time is important for the creative process. I sometimes remark as I hand my wife a copy of my sermon, "This is draft fifteen!" That may be a bit of hyperbole, but my exaggeration is often not far off. Good sermons require editing.

Oral Language

The use of oral language is essential. Preaching is an oral medium and not strictly a literary one. The sermon may be written, but it should be written using oral language. I have found it helpful to do much of my preparation aloud. In doing that, I can hear how what I have written sounds. This helps to insure the use of oral language. In writing an essay we guard against sentence fragments and repetition. But in oral language sentence fragments are often fine and repetition is essential. Good preachers know how to write using the language of orality.

I once read a sermon by John Piper. And then a little later I had opportunity to hear a recording of the same sermon. I was surprised by how different they were. In the oral sermon there were digressions, incomplete sentences and amplifications that were not found in the written sermon. We always speak differently than we write. We who preach should learn to write using the language of orality.

A Plan to Follow

The developmental process described in this chapter will not replace the hard work of shaping thought. The developmental process will always be an uphill journey. What the process gives us is direction for the trip. It gives us a plan to follow. And having a plan can move us away from sermon gridlock toward the wonderful freedom of the Spirit of God.

And so we conclude this homiletic journey. The road has not always been clear. There were twists and turns. The product may not always be polished. But in the end we have a sermon, a word from above. And we have attempted to present that word in as creative and interesting a way as we can. To God be the glory.

Epilogue

Pastor Bill sits at his desk pondering his journey into the world of contemporary homiletic design. For eighteen months he has read and explored and experimented with creative approaches to the old task. He has read about deductive, narrative, inductive, story, and even phenomenological-move sermons. And he has attempted quite a few of them.

His attempts at narrative preaching have gone better than expected. *I guess everyone loves a story,* he thinks. He risked a first-person narrative at Christmastime (resisting the temptation to dress the part!). That had been well received. Numerous times he has taken a more inductive approach to his sermon design. And then there was that attempt at story preaching. *Can't win them all,* he smiles to himself.

Pastor Bill still favors more deductive forms—the subject-completed form is his favorite! He just feels most comfortable with the deductive approach. But now he knows there are other options.

The work of sermon design is still a hard task. He often finds himself staring at a blank sheet of paper, wondering how to design this sermon. But sermonic gridlock seems to happen less often now. And he finds his way clear more quickly.

It has been quite a trip, he muses. But then he realizes that the journey is not over, it is really just beginning. . . .

Appendix A

DESIGNING THE BASIC FORM

- **Step 1: Begin with the Sermon Focus**

  Subject:

  Complement:

  Homiletical Idea:

  Purpose:

- **Step 2: Do a Structural Analysis of the Text**

  What are the major blocks of thought in the text?

  Write a one-sentence description for each.

- **Step 3: Do an Audience Analysis**

  What questions will my audience raise?

  What will they not understand?

- **Step 4: Complete a Sermon Task List**

  What needs to be said and done in this sermon to fulfill my sermon focus?

- **Step 5: Select and Sequence the Thought**

  What are the main thoughts from my sermon task list that will make up the structure of this sermon?

  How will I sequence those thoughts?

Appendix B

CONSIDERING STANDARD FORMS

What structure will my sermon use?

- **Deductive Sermon Structure**

  Will my big idea be given in the introduction or the first point?

  What developmental question will be used to explore the big idea?

- **Semi-Deductive Sermon Structure (Subject-Completed)**

  This structure is used when there are multiple complements.

  What are the complements for this sermon?

- **Inductive Sermon Structure**

  Write out the main points or movements for the sermon structure.

  What is the logical order for the structure?

- **Inductive/Deductive Sermon Structure**

  Where in the sermon will the full statement of the homiletical idea be given?

  What developmental question will be used to develop the deductive portion of the sermon?

Appendix C

DESIGNING NARRATIVE SERMONS

- **Step 1: Begin with the Sermon Focus**

  Subject:

  Complement:

  Homiletical Idea:

  Purpose:

- **Step 2: Do a Plot Analysis**

  Break the narrative into sections or scenes.

  Write out a brief summary for each section or scene.

- **Step 3: Notice Any Literary Devices or Features**

  What literary devices or features (chiasm, repetition, direct discourse, etc.) does the narrative employ?

  With whom does the author intend the reader to identify?

- **Step 4: Do an Audience Analysis**

  What questions will my audience raise?

  What will they not understand?

- **Step 5: Complete a Sermon Task List**

  What needs to be said and done in this sermon to fulfill my sermon focus?

- **Step 6: Replot the Text in Terms of the Sermon**

  What are the main thoughts from my sermon task list that will make up the structure of this sermon?

  How will I sequence those thoughts?

  Will my sermon follow the plot of the narrative? Why or why not?

Appendix D

EXPANDING THE SERMON FORM

- **Step 1: Do a Homiletic Analysis for Each Main Point**

  Opening Statement:

  Biblical Support:

  Theology:

  Congregational Objections:

  Images, Examples, Illustrations:

- **Step 2: Write a Beginning Draft**

  Opening:

  Development:

  Close:

- **Step 3: Add Transitions**

  Write out a transitional phrase or sentence for each main point.

- **Step 4: Develop the Final Form**

  Write out a manuscript or complete outline for the entire sermon.

NOTES

Chapter 1 Introduction to Sermon Form

1. Eugene L. Lowry, "The Revolution of Sermonic Shape," in *Listening to the Word*, ed. Gail R. O'Day and Thomas G. Long (Nashville: Abingdon, 1993), 95.

2. Richard L. Eslinger, *A New Hearing: Living Options in Homiletic Method* (Nashville: Abingdon, 1987), 65.

3. Halford E. Luccock, *In the Minister's Workshop* (New York: Abingdon, 1944), 118.

4. Thomas G. Long, "Form," in *Concise Encyclopedia of Preaching*, ed. William H. Willimon and Richard Lischer (Louisville: Westminster John Knox, 1995), 144.

5. Ralph L. Lewis and Gregg Lewis, *Inductive Preaching* (Wheaton: Crossway, 1983), 35.

6. Long, "Form," 147.

7. Fred B. Craddock, *As One without Authority*, 3rd ed. (Nashville: Abingdon, 1979), 51–75.

8. Sidney Greidanus, *Preaching Christ from the Old Testament* (Grand Rapids: Eerdmans, 1999), 8.

Chapter 2 The Shapes That Sermons Take

1. I use the terms *classical* and *traditional* interchangeably to refer to the sermon structures prevalent during the first half of the twentieth century.

2. Luccock, *In the Minister's Workshop*, 134–47.

3. Long, "Form," 146.

4. Henry Grady Davis, *Design for Preaching* (Philadelphia: Muhlenberg, 1958), 175.

5. Long, "Form," 147.

6. Lewis and Lewis, *Inductive Preaching*, 35.

7. Craddock, *As One without Authority*, 1–21.

8. Ibid., 14.

9. Charles L. Campbell, "Inductive Preaching," in *Concise Encyclopedia of Preaching*, ed. William H. Willimon and Richard Lischer (Louisville: Westminster John Knox, 1995), 272.

10. Davis, *Design for Preaching*, 175–77.

11. Eugene L. Lowry, *The Homiletical Plot: The Sermon as Narrative Art Form* (Atlanta: John Knox, 1980), 23.

12. Craddock, *As One without Authority*, 57.

13. Ibid., 152.

14. Ibid., 58.

15. Ibid., 64.

16. Ibid., 62.

17. Ibid., 163–68.

18. Haddon W. Robinson, *Biblical Preaching*, 2nd ed. (Grand Rapids: Baker, 2001), 127.

19. Lowry, "Revolution of Sermonic Shape," 110–11.

20. Campbell, "Inductive Preaching," 271.

21. Craddock, *As One without Authority*, 125.

22. Gordon Fee and Douglas Stuart note that the Old Testament is over 40 percent narrative. Gordon D. Fee and Douglas Stuart, *How to Read the Bible for All Its Worth*, 3rd ed. (Grand Rapids: Zondervan, 2003), 89.

23. Ibid., 3.

24. Ibid., 61.

25. Thomas G. Long, "And How Shall They Hear? The Listener in Contemporary Preaching" in *Listening to the Word*, ed. Gail R. O'Day and Thomas G. Long (Nashville: Abingdon, 1993), 187.

26. David Buttrick, *Homiletic* (Philadelphia: Fortress, 1987), 293.

27. Fred Craddock, "Say and Do," in *The Art and Craft of Biblical Preaching*, ed. Haddon Robinson and Craig Brian Larson (Grand Rapids: Zondervan, 2005), 327.

28. Calvin Miller, *The Empowered Communicator* (Nashville: Broadman & Holman, 1994), 100.

29. Craddock, *As One without Authority*, 53.

30. John S. McClure, "Narrative and Preachers: Sorting It All Out," *Journal for Preachers* 15, no. 1 (Advent 1991): 25.

31. Eugene Lowry, "Narrative Preaching," in *Concise Encyclopedia of Preaching*, ed. William H. Willimon and Richard Lischer (Louisville: Westminster John Knox, 1995), 342.

32. Thomas G. Long, "Shaping Sermons by Plotting the Text's Claim upon Us," in *Preaching Biblically*, ed. Don M. Wardlaw (Philadelphia: Westminster, 1983), 87.

33. Lowry, "Narrative Preaching," 343.

34. Ibid., 342.

35. Amos N. Wilder, *Early Christian Rhetoric: The Language of the Gospel* (1964; repr., Cambridge: Harvard University Press, 1971). Original edition was published by Harper & Row under the title *The Language of the Gospel: Early Christian Rhetoric*. Citations are from the 1971 edition.

36. Stephen Crites, "The Narrative Quality of Experience," *Journal of the American Academy of Religion* 39 (September 1971): 291.

37. Lowry, "Revolution of Sermonic Shape," 96–97.

38. Ibid., 101–5.

39. Ibid., 107.

40. Ibid., 108.

41. Ibid., 110.

42. Ibid., 111.

43. Lowry, *The Homiletical Plot*, 29.

44. Eugene L. Lowry, *The Sermon: Dancing the Edge of Mystery* (Nashville: Abingdon, 1997), 62.

45. Thomas G. Long, *The Witness of Preaching* (Louisville: Westminster/John Knox, 1989), 36–37.

46. Richard Lischer, "Preaching and the Rhetoric of Promise," *Word and World* 8, no. 1 (Winter 1988): 79.

47. Lowry, "Narrative Preaching," 342.

48. Edmund A. Steimle, Morris J. Niedenthal, and Charles L. Rice, *Preaching the Story* (Philadelphia: Fortress, 1980).

49. Richard A. Jensen, *Telling the Story: Variety and Imagination in Preaching* (Minneapolis: Augsburg, 1980); idem., *Thinking in Story: Preaching in a Post-Literate Age* (Lima, OH: CSS Publishing, 1993).

50. Steimle, Niedenthal, and Rice, *Preaching the Story*, 12–13.

51. Robinson, *Biblical Preaching*, 129.

52. Mark Ellingsen, *The Integrity of Biblical Narrative: Story in Theology and Proclamation* (Minneapolis: Fortress, 1990), 8.

53. Richard Lischer, "The Limits of Story," *Interpretation* 38 (January 1, 1984): 26–38.

54. Ibid., 35.

55. Ibid., 36.

56. Long, *The Witness of Preaching*, 40.

57. Ibid.

58. Ibid., 41.

59. William H. Willimon, "Stories and Sermons," *Christian Ministry* 14, no. 6 (1983): 6.

60. Ellingsen, *Integrity of Biblical Narrative*, 8.

61. Paul Scott Wilson, *The Four Pages of the Sermon: A Guide to Biblical Preaching* (Nashville: Abingdon, 1999), 156.

62. Ibid., 16.

63. Frederick Buechner, *Telling the Truth: The Gospel as Tragedy, Comedy, and Fairy Tale* (San Francisco: Harper & Row, 1977), 7.

64. Bryan Chapell, *Christ-Centered Preaching: Redeeming the Expository Sermon*, 2nd ed. (Grand Rapids: Baker, 2005), 50.

65. Ibid., 272.

66. Buttrick, *Homiletic*, xi.

67. Ibid., 23.

68. Ibid., 26.

69. Ibid., 38.

70. Ibid., 51.

71. Ibid., 39.
72. Ibid., 41, 42.
73. Ibid., 47.
74. Ibid., 51.
75. Ibid., 71.
76. Ibid.
77. Ibid., 79.
78. John S. McClure, "Theories of Language," in *Concise Encyclopedia of Preaching*, ed. William H. Willimon and Richard Lischer (Louisville: Westminster John Knox, 1995), 293.
79. Ibid., 308.
80. Ibid., 313.
81. Ibid., 316.
82. Ibid., 313.
83. Long, *The Witness of Preaching*, 104.

Chapter 3 The Theology of Design

1. Long, "Form," 144.
2. Karl Barth, *Homiletics*, trans. Geoffrey W. Bromiley and Donald E. Daniels (Louisville: Westminster/John Knox, 1991), 121.
3. Long, "Form," 145.
4. Richard Lischer, "Preaching as the Church's Language" in *Listening to the Word*, ed. Gail R. O'Day and Thomas G. Long (Nashville: Abingdon, 1993), 122.
5. Long, "Form" 145.
6. Ibid.
7. Davis, *Design for Preaching*, 3.
8. Thomas G. Long, interview by author, August 6, 1996, Princeton Theological Seminary, Princeton, New Jersey.
9. Lischer, "Preaching as the Church's Language," 128.
10. Craddock, *As One without Authority*, 3.
11. Lischer, "Preaching and the Rhetoric of Promise," 69.
12. McClure, "Theories of Language," 292.
13. Ibid., 293.
14. Ibid.
15. Ibid., 294.
16. Buttrick, *Homiletic*, 184.
17. Chapell, *Christ-Centered Preaching*, 136.
18. George A. Lindbeck, *The Nature of Doctrine: Religion and Theology in a Postliberal Age* (Philadelphia: Westminster, 1984), 16.
19. Ibid.
20. David James Randolph, *The Renewal of Preaching* (Philadelphia: Fortress, 1969), 1 (emphasis added).
21. Long, *The Witness of Preaching*, 84.
22. Robinson, *Biblical Preaching*, 107.

Chapter 4 Literary Concerns and Sermon Form

1. John Collins, "Towards the Morphology of a Genre," *Semeia* 14 (1979): 1.

2. Sidney Greidanus, *The Modern Preacher and the Ancient Text: Interpreting and Preaching Biblical Literature* (Grand Rapids: Eerdmans, 1988), 23.

3. Ibid.

4. Thomas G. Long, *Preaching and the Literary Forms of the Bible* (Philadelphia: Fortress, 1989), 12.

5. Wilder, *Early Christian Rhetoric*, 25.

6. Craddock, *As One without Authority*, 45.

7. John C. Holbert, *Preaching Old Testament: Proclamation and Narrative in the Hebrew Bible* (Nashville: Abingdon, 1991), 47.

8. Henry Mitchell, "The Hearer's Experience of the Word" in *Listening to the Word*, ed. Gail R. O'Day and Thomas G. Long (Nashville: Abingdon, 1993), 233.

9. Fred B. Craddock, *Preaching* (Nashville: Abingdon, 1985), 178.

10. Greidanus, *The Modern Preacher*, 141.

11. Ronald Allen, "Shaping Sermons by the Language of the Text," in *Preaching Biblically*, ed. Don M. Wardlaw (Philadelphia: Westminster, 1983), 35.

12. Long, *Preaching and the Literary Forms of the Bible*, 24.

13. Much contemporary parable scholarship would contest the idea that parables have a single point, instead arguing for the polyvalence of parables. I would still hold that parables often have a single focus.

14. O. C. Edwards Jr., "History of Preaching," in *Concise Encyclopedia of Preaching*, ed. William H. Willimon and Richard Lischer (Louisville: Westminster John Knox, 1995), 185.

15. I am indebted to D. A. Carson for this distinction. D. A. Carson, "Matthew," *Expositor's Bible Commentary* (Grand Rapids: Zondervan, 1984), 8:124.

16. I am indebted to Timothy Slemmons, interim pastor at First Presbyterian Church in Titusville, New Jersey, and visiting lecturer at Princeton Theological Seminary for this insight shared with me fall 2005.

17. Campbell, "Inductive Preaching," 271.

18. Donald Sunukjian, "Patterns for Preaching—A Rhetorical Analysis of the Sermons of Paul in Acts 13, 17, and 20" (Th.D. diss., Dallas Theological Seminary, 1972), 181–82.

Chapter 5 Culture and Sermon Form

1. Craddock, *As One without Authority*, 12.

2. Jeffrey D. Arthurs, "The Postmodern Mind and Preaching" in *Preaching to a Shifting Culture*, ed. Scott M. Gibson (Grand Rapids: Baker, 2004), 177.

3. D. A. Carson, *Becoming Conversant with the Emerging Church: Understanding a Movement and Its Implications* (Grand Rapids: Zondervan, 2005), 75.

4. Calvin Miller, *Marketplace Preaching: How to Return the Sermon to Where It Belongs* (Grand Rapids: Baker, 1995), 19.

5. Ibid., 65.

6. Michael J. Quicke, *360-Degree Preaching: Hearing, Speaking, and Living the Word* (Grand Rapids: Baker, 2003), 72.

7. Wade Clark Roof, *A Generation of Seekers* (San Francisco: HarperSan-Francisco, 1993), 50.

8. Ibid., 53.

9. Ibid., 36.

10. Ibid., 50.

11. Ibid., 54.

12. Ibid.

13. Walter J. Ong, *The Presence of the Word: Some Prolegomena for Cultural and Religious History* (New Haven: Yale University Press, 1967), 17.

14. Walter J. Ong cited in Quentin J. Schultze, "Television and Preaching," in *Concise Encyclopedia of Preaching*, ed. William H. Willimon and Richard Lischer (Louisville: Westminster John Knox, 1995), 473.

15. Ong, *The Presence of the Word*, 88.

16. Schultze, "Television and Preaching," 473.

17. Quicke, *360-Degree Preaching*, 79.

18. Ibid., 81.

19. Barbara Bates, "Oral Communication and Preaching" in *Concise Encyclopedia of Preaching*, ed. William H. Willimon and Richard Lischer (Louisville: Westminster John Knox, 1995), 353.

20. Kathleen Hall Jamieson, *Eloquence in an Electronic Age: The Transformation of Political Speechmaking* (New York: Oxford University Press, 1988), 137.

21. Marshall McLuhan and Quentin Fiore, *The Medium Is the Message* (New York: Bantam Books, 1967), 125.

22. Craddock, *As One without Authority*, 62.

23. Roof, *A Generation of Seekers*, 54.

24. Schultz, "Television and Preaching," 471.

25. Kathleen Hall Jamieson, *Eloquence in an Electronic Age*, cited in Arthurs, "The Postmodern Mind and Preaching," 194.

26. Quicke, *360-Degree Preaching*, 73.

27. Graham Johnston, *Preaching to a Postmodern World: A Guide to Reaching Twenty-First Century Listeners* (Grand Rapids: Baker, 2001), 149–72.

28. Don Sunukjian, cited in Haddon Robinson, "Preaching to Everyone in Particular," in *The Art and Craft of Biblical Preaching*, ed. Haddon Robinson and Craig Brian Larson (Grand Rapids: Zondervan, 2005), 117.

29. In Leonora Tubbs Tisdale, *Preaching as Local Theology and Folk Art* (Minneapolis: Fortress, 1997), Tisdale has a helpful chapter titled, "Exegeting the Congregation," 56–90. In it she suggests seven symbols for congregational exegesis: stories and interviews, archival materials, demographics, architecture and visual arts, rituals, events and activities, and people.

Chapter 6 An Evangelical Approach

1. Robinson, *Biblical Preaching*, 131.

2. Craddock, *Preaching*, 182.

3. Haddon Robinson, "Set Free from the Cookie Cutter," in *The Art and Craft of Biblical Preaching*, ed. Haddon Robinson and Craig Brian Larson (Grand Rapids: Zondervan, 2005), 323.

4. Craddock, *Preaching*, 173–74.

5. Calvin Miller, "Narrative Preaching," in *Handbook of Contemporary Preaching*, ed. Michael Duduit (Nashville: Broadman, 1992), 108.

Chapter 7 Identifying the Sermon Focus

1. Haddon Robinson, "Better Big Ideas," in *The Art and Craft of Biblical Preaching*, ed. Haddon Robinson and Craig Brian Larson (Grand Rapids: Zondervan, 2005), 355.
2. Robinson, *Biblical Preaching*, 33.
3. John Koessler, "View from the Pew," in *The Art and Craft of Biblical Preaching*, ed. Haddon Robinson and Craig Brian Larson (Grand Rapids: Zondervan, 2005), 124.
4. Davis, *Design for Preaching*, 20.
5. Long, *The Witness of Preaching*, 86.
6. Robinson, "Better Big Ideas," 356.
7. Ibid., 357.
8. Bill Hybels, "Leading, Teaching, and Having a Life," (message, Willow Creek Community Church, South Barrington, Illinois, October 18, 2004).
9. Robert F. Mager, *Preparing Instructional Objectives* (Belmont, CA: Lake Publishing Company, 1984), 20.

Chapter 8 Designing the Basic Form

1. Chapell, *Christ-Centered Preaching*, 162.
2. Long, *The Witness of Preaching*, 93.
3. Ibid., 94.
4. Greidanus, *The Modern Preacher*, 141.
5. Craddock, *Preaching*, 174.
6. Robinson, *Biblical Preaching*, 116.
7. Ibid., 75.
8. H. Grady Davis talks about these three questions in *Design for Preaching*, 24–25. He calls them functional questions. They are developed further by Robinson, *Biblical Preaching*, 75–96.
9. Craddock, "Say and Do," 328.
10. Probably the best text on how genre should influence the sermon is Thomas Long, *Preaching and the Literary Forms of the Bible*. Long speaks of interrogating the text and asks five questions: (1) What is the genre of the text? (2) What is the rhetorical function of this genre? (3) What literary device does this genre employ to achieve its rhetorical effect? (4) How in particular does the text under consideration, in its own literary setting, embody the characteristics and dynamics described in the previous questions? And (5) How may the sermon, in a new setting, say and do what the text says and does in its setting? These five questions are intended to help the preacher see how the form of the text can influence the sermon. Long says, "The preacher's task, though, is not to replicate the text but to regenerate the impact of some portion of the text" (33). Long includes helpful chapters on preaching psalms, proverbs, narratives, parables, and epistles (see 43–126).
11. Long, *The Witness of Preaching*, 107.

12. Chapell, *Christ-Centered Preaching*, 269–95.

13. Wilson, *The Four Pages of the Sermon*, 16.

14. Long, *The Witness of Preaching*, 108.

Chapter 9 Considering Standard Forms

1. Lowry, *The Homiletical Plot*, 29.

2. Robinson, *Biblical Preaching*, 118–23.

3. Campbell, "Inductive Preaching," 270.

4. Don Sunukjian, "The Tension Between Clarity and Suspense," in *The Art and Craft of Biblical Preaching*, ed. Haddon Robinson and Craig Brian Larson (Grand Rapids: Zondervan, 2005), 364.

5. William E. Sangster, "He Dies. He Must Die," in *Classic Sermons on the Cross of Christ*, ed. Warren W. Wiersbe (Grand Rapids: Hendrickson, 1990), 25–32.

6. Campbell, "Inductive Preaching," 270.

7. Miller, *Marketplace Preaching*, 65.

8. Craig Brian Larson, "The Power of Sequence," in *The Art and Craft of Biblical Preaching*, ed. Haddon Robinson and Craig Brian Larson (Grand Rapids: Zondervan, 2005), 358–60.

9. Paul Scott Wilson, *Preaching and Homiletical Theory* (St. Louis: Chalice, 2004), 94.

10. Chapell, *Christ-Centered Preaching*, 48.

11. Lowry, *The Sermon*, 66.

12. Wilson, *Preaching and Homiletical Theory*, 94.

13. Chapell, *Christ-Centered Preaching*, 269–95.

14. Robinson, *Biblical Preaching*, 126.

15. Stephen F. Olford, *The Pulpit and the Christian Calendar: Preaching on Significant Days* (Grand Rapids: Baker, 1991), 82–88.

Chapter 10 Preaching the Narrative Genre

1. Greidanus, *The Modern Preacher*, 23.

2. Calvin Miller, *Preaching: The Art of Narrative Exposition* (Grand Rapids: Baker, 2006), 65.

3. Long, *Literary Forms*, 33.

4. Greidanus, *The Modern Preacher*, 188.

5. Long, *Literary Forms*, 66.

6. For help with preaching other genres, see Long, *Literary Forms*.

7. Haddon W. Robinson, "The Relevance of Expository Preaching," in *Preaching to a Shifting Culture*, ed. Scott M. Gibson (Grand Rapids: Baker, 2004), 87–88.

8. Long, *Literary Forms*, 71.

9. Ibid., 74.

10. Lowry, "Narrative Preaching," 342.

11. Davis, *Design for Preaching*, 157.

12. Miller, "Narrative Preaching," 103.

13. Greidanus, *The Modern Preacher*, 151.

14. Allen, "Shaping Sermons by the Language of the Text," 34.

15. Paul Borden and Steven D. Mathewson, "The Big Idea of Narrative Preaching," in *The Art and Craft of Biblical Preaching*, ed. Haddon Robinson and Craig Brian Larson (Grand Rapids: Zondervan, 2005), 274–78.

16. Ibid., 278–79.

17. Robert Alter, *The Art of Biblical Narrative* (New York: Basic Books, 1981), 180.

18. Robert Alter, *The World of Biblical Literature* (New York: Basic Books, 1992), 74.

19. Eugene L. Lowry, *How to Preach a Parable: Designs for Narrative Sermons* (Nashville: Abingdon, 1989), 38.

20. Holbert, *Preaching Old Testament*, 42.

21. Ibid., 43.

22. Calvin Miller, "Encounter at Jabbok," *Preaching Today*, audio tape 153 (Carol Stream, IL: Christianity Today International, 1996).

23. Holbert, *Preaching Old Testament*, 43.

24. Quicke, *360-Degree Preaching*, 204–9.

25. Adapted from class notes developed by Haddon W. Robinson, Gordon-Conwell Theological Seminary. Also see Haddon W. Robinson and Torrey W. Robinson, *It's All in How You Tell It: Preaching First-Person Expository Messages* (Grand Rapids: Baker, 2003).

Chapter 11 Expanding the Sermon Form

1. I acknowledge David Buttrick's influence on me for this idea. However, the approach is not wholly original with Buttrick since most preachers do something like this intuitively as they write the sermon. What is being advocated here is that such an analysis be done for each main point *before* writing the sermon draft. Buttrick, *Homiletic*, 49.

2. Ibid., 337–39.

3. Ibid., 114.

4. Long, *The Witness of Preaching*, 148.

5. Chapell, *Christ-Centered Preaching*, 156.

6. Ibid., 158–59.

7. David L. Larsen, *The Anatomy of Preaching: Identifying the Issues in Preaching Today* (Grand Rapids: Kregel, 1989), 62.

8. Buttrick, *Homiletic*, 160.

9. Duane Litfin, *Public Speaking: A Handbook for Christians*, 2nd ed. (Grand Rapids: Baker, 1992), 189.

10. Buttrick, *Homiletic*, 69–79.

Dennis M. Cahill (D.Min., Gordon-Conwell Theological Seminary) has been in the pastorate for more than twenty years. He is the founding pastor of Christ Community Church, a Bible Fellowship Church in New Jersey, and is active in the Evangelical Homiletical Society.